Pain Control

Second edition

Jane Latham

Austen Cornish Publishers Limited
in association with
The Lisa Sainsbury Foundation

First edition published in 1987 by
Austen Cornish Publishers Limited,
in association with
The Lisa Sainsbury Foundation

ISBN 1 870065 16 6

Printed in Great Britain by MRM Associates Ltd,
322 Oxford Road, Reading, Berks.

Contents

Foreword

This second edition comes at a most opportune time because the subject is advancing rapidly and the demands on nurses increase and therefore the opportunities and responsibilities of nurses increase. Nurses emerge from an era of passive servitude at a time when medicine is in crisis. That crisis originates from the increasingly evident fact that no country in the world can afford the medical services required by its citizens if existing financial and professional organisations persist. In the resolution of that crisis, it will be inevitable that nurses will emerge with a leadership responsibility. That will require a higher level of education than has been accepted in the past. This book is an example of the new generation which is urgently required.

It is apparent that our understanding of pain mechanisms advances rapidly. That does not mean that pain becomes a precise predictable phenomenon. Pain is not exactly related to the amount of damaged tissue and to the nature of the damage. Pain is an expression of the overall reaction of the whole person who happens to have some damaged tissue. That means that it is necessary to be close to the patient as a whole in order to assess and to treat pain. No one is in a better position to understand that need for subtlety than the nurse.

Nurses, like the rest of us, are both victims and exponents of sexism, ageism and other forms of bias. There is a terrible urge, especially when in a hurry, to assign an appropriate amount of pain to a particular condition. This tendency gives a patient permission to complain of a certain level of pain, no more and no less. We assign an additional label to 'macho men', 'scruffy little boys', 'little old ladies' and, of course, 'foreigners'. Their label is a measure of the credibility we attach to their complaint. That is all wrong. No amount of science is going to substitute for the need to assess the individual as an individual and not as a disease or as a stereotype. Science gives the power to understand and control general processes. It also emphasises that there is not one pain mechanism but a sequential series which take over one from the other and mould the nervous system into new organisations as time passes. Attention naturally focusses on the initiating disease process. That must not be the only focus because the disease exists in an individual who is reacting. Of all therapists, the nurse is in the most crucial position to play a part in that reaction.

Professor Patrick D. Wall, FRS DM FRCP
London, October 1990

Preface

The first edition of this book provided a theoretical and clinical background in pain control which could be applied to everyday practice, offering colleagues throughout the health care professions new insight into the wide range of techniques and skills that exist. Due to the fact that developments in the field of pain control are taking place so rapidly, the second edition of this book aims to continue the theme of the first edition by updating key areas relating to clinical practice.

This short book therefore continues to provide readers throughout the caring professions with the confidence and knowledge to face up to the pain their patients experience and to provide better and quicker support and treatment for those patients.

Jane Latham
London, August 1990

Preface to the first edition

The aim of this book is to provide a thoretical and clinical background in pain control which can be applied to everyday practice. I am particularly concerned to offer my colleagues throughout the health care professions new insight into the wide range of techniques and skills which now exist, and which continue to develop rapidly, to enable them to treat pain more effectively and quickly than is often the case in current practice. I hope, also, that this book will provide a point of reference should readers wish to study other aspects of pain control not as yet commonly met in everyday practice such as alternative methods of pain control.

I feel strongly that accurate and continuing assessment of the pain of each individual patient is of prime importance when deciding on the most appropriate forms of both initial and follow-up treatment, and in Chapter 4, I examine some of the tools which are readily available to us for such work. Only with consistent and continuing assessment can we really have a clear picture of the nature and degree of our patients' pain.

Perhaps health care professionals sometimes hesitate to acknowledge that their patients experience pain at all because they are at a loss to know how best to offer them effective treatment. I hope that this short book will provide readers throughout the caring professions with the confidence and knowledge to face up to the pain their patients *do* experience, and to provide better and quicker support and treatment for them.

Jane Latham
London, August 1987

Acknowledgements

Colleagues from several disciplines have been invaluable in offering both ideas and support during the writing of this book. I would particularly like to thank: Maureen Williams, Principal Clinical Psychologist, Pain Relief Unit, King's College Hospital, for contributing Chapter 5; Susan Burton, Chief Pharmacist, King's College Hospital, for her ideas and guidance on Chapter 6; Dr Magdi Hanna, Consultant, Pain Relief Unit, King's College Hospital, for his constructive criticism throughout; and Thelma Calnan for secretarial support.

The authors and publishers are grateful to the following for permission to reproduce or adapt material:

Penguin Books Ltd and Dr R. Melzack and Professor P. Wall, Figures 2.2 and 3.4; Science and Dr R. Melzack and Professor P. Wall, Figure 3.3; Camberwell Health Authority, Figure 4.3; Springhouse Corporation, Figure 4.4; Churchill Livingstone, Table 5.1; Hodder & Stoughton and Professor Crisp, Table 5.3; Elsevier Biomedical Press BV, Table 5.4 and Figure 5.5; Graseby Medical, Figure 7.2; B. Braun Medical Ltd, Figure 7.3; Abbott Laboratories Ltd, Figure 7.4; Bard Ltd, Figure 7.5; N.H. Eastwood & Son Ltd, Figure 9.2; and Research Press Inc. and D.A. Berstein and T.O. Borkover, text on pages 49–52.

Functional anatomy and physiology of pain 1

An overview of the functional anatomy and physiology of pain is useful background knowledge that can be used as a reference point when subjects such as pain theories, assessment of pain and treatment of pain are being discussed in future chapters.

THALAMUS AND CEREBRAL CORTEX

The thalamus is a relay station where crude, uncritical sensations reach the consciousness. Finer sensations are thought to be transmitted to the cerebral cortex. That pain reaches consciousness in the thalamus is shown by the fact that it can be felt when all connections have been severed between the thalamus and the cortex. The cortex may, however, play a part in the modality of pain. The connections between the thalamus, cortex and pain are still under investigation.

SPINAL NERVES

There are 31 pairs of spinal nerves named according to the level at which they emerge from the neural canal. Five large nerve plexuses are formed on each side of the vertebral column.

Nerve plexuses arise from both sides of the spinal cord and are numbered according to the level of the spinal cord at which they emerge from the intervertebral foramen. They are mixed sensory and motor nerves.

Sympathetic ganglia arise from both sides of the spinal cord and are numbered according to the level at which they emerge on the spinal cord. Fibres pass out of the spinal cord with the anterior nerve routes (see Fig. 1.1).

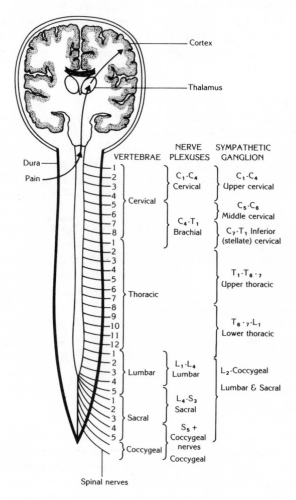

Fig. 1.1 A diagrammatic view of the spinal cord showing the relationship between the vertebrae, nerve plexuses and sympathetic ganglia.

Cervical plexus (C_1–C_4)
Some of the nerves that emerge from this plexus are the phrenic nerve, sensory nerves to the skin of the neck and back of the scalp and motor nerves to the muscles of the neck.

Brachial plexus (C4–T1)
This is situated above and behind the subclavian vessels and also partly in the axilla. The arm and axilla are supplied by five large nerves which are the circumflex, radial, musculocutaneous, median and ulnar nerves.

Lumbar plexus (L1–part of L4)
The femoral and obturator nerves which supply the thigh and the knee emerge from this plexus.

Sacral plexus (Part of L4–S3)
The sciatic nerve emerges from this plexus, and its branches supply the lower leg. Nerves from this plexus also supply the perineum.

Coccygeal plexus (S5 and coccygeal nerves)
The twelve pairs of thoracic nerves do not form a plexus because each pair passes between the ribs to form the intercostal nerves.

AUTONOMIC NERVOUS SYSTEM

Sympathetic system

The sympathetic nervous system has special connections in the lateral horn of grey matter of the thoracic and upper lumbar sections of the spinal cord.

Ganglia
Fibres pass with the anterior nerve roots out of the spinal cord and end on each side in a chain of six ganglia which are linked together. A ganglion is a group of fibres from both sides of the body in close proximity to each other which synapse on to each other in such a way that information is sorted and selected. The activity of a ganglion is therefore much like that of a relay station. The chain of ganglia is made up of:

1. Upper cervical ganglion
2. Middle cervical ganglion
3. Inferior cervical ganglion

4.   Upper thoracic ganglion
5.   Lower thoracic ganglion
6.   Lumbar and sacral ganglia.
(see Fig.1.1)

Plexuses
At the structures and vessels supplied by these nerves large and complex nerve plexuses are formed, these include:

1.   Coeliac plexus   This supplies the upper abdominal organs such as the stomach, pancreas, liver, gall bladder and upper colon.
2.   Lumbar plexus   This supplies the lower abdominal organs and lower limbs.

Ascending pathways
The ascending nerve pathways are arranged within the spinal cord in a segmental lamination which systematically reflects the different organ segments from which they originate.

Parasympathetic system

The parasympathetic nervous system emerges from the central nervous system in two quite separate areas. Both areas have their central connection in the cerebral cortex and hypothalamus.

Cranial area
This leaves the brain in the oculomotor, facial, glossopharyngeal, vagus and accessory nerves.

Sacral area
Fibres arise from cells in the lateral grey columns of S_2–S_4 and the pelvic splanchnic nerves.

PAIN FIBRES

Pain is perceived in two waves:

1.   Distinct and brief
2.   Diffuse and aching

This concept is illustrated in Fig.1.2 and results from the transmission of pain impulses along two types of nerve fibre at differing speeds.

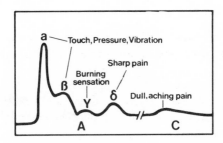

Fig. 1.2 Verbal reports of the sensations evoked by stimulation of different groups of nerve fibres.

When assessing pain, it is essential for nurses to understand that different nerve fibres are involved in the transmission of pain; this diagram shows how the different excitation of various fibres is experienced.

A fibres

These are rapidly conducting fibres which are thought to give rise to sensations of distinct, sharp, well-defined and localised pain closely related to the time at which a sharp external stimulus is received.

C fibres

These are thin, slowly conducting fibres, which are thought to give experience of diffuse, unpleasant and unbearable pain.

SYNAPSES

There is no anatomical continuity between one neuron and another. At the free end of one neuron, the axon divides into minute branches called 'end feet'. These end feet are in close proximity to the dendrites or cell body of the next neuron.

Chemical transmitters

Stimulation of the next neuron is activated by short-lived chemical transmitters which are neutralised by the enzyme cholinesterase and rendered inactive when they have stimulated the next neuron.

In all ganglia, both sympathetic and parasympathetic, acetylcholine is the chemical transmitter produced at the arrival of the stimulus. This is also produced at the second set of parasympathetic fibres at the nerve endings.

Noradrenaline is the chemical transmitter produced at the nerve endings of the second set of sympathetic fibres. However, noradrenaline release may be stimulated by an initial production of acetylcholine.

PAIN IMPULSES

First neuron fibre
This enters the spinal cord by a posterior nerve root and ends by synapsing in the posterior horn of grey matter.

Second neuron fibre
This begins in a cell in the posterior horn, crosses immediately over to the other side of the spinal cord and ascends as the lateral spinothalamic tract, to synapse in the thalamus.

Third neuron fibre
This has its cell in the thalamus and passes to the sensory area in the parietal cortex. Fig.1.3 shows a typical pain pathway in which three nerve fibres are involved.

CHEMICAL PAIN MEDIATORS

Chemical pain mediators are thought to be released when an inflammatory process occurs. Enhancement or block of their action can therefore potentially alter the way pain is mediated.

Examples of these chemicals are:

1. Bradykinin   This is rapidly broken down and is probably involved in the action of acute pain.

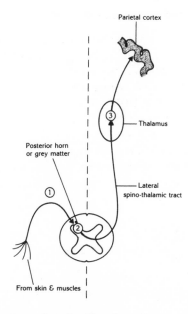

Fig. 1.3   Pain pathways from the skin and muscles to the parietal cortex.

2.   Prostaglandins   These are synthesised at the site of inflammation and sensitise the pain fibre endings, thus enhancing pain. They induce the effect of bradykinin.

3.   Substance P is thought to be produced when noxious peripheral stimuli activate dorsal horn neurons. Substance P therefore appears to be the neurotransmitter substance released by small primary afferents which transmit painful stimuli.

4.   5-Hydroxytryptamine (5HT)

5.   Noradrenaline

6.   Histamine

MODIFICATION OF PAIN

Although a painful stimulus activates the relevant pain pathways, the information carried by them can become modified within the nervous system. These mechanisms and their implications for pain control will be discussed in more detail in future chapters.

BIBLIOGRAPHY

Gibson, J. (1974) *A Guide to the Nervous System*. Faber and Faber, London. (An excellent guide to the nervous system.)

Latham, J. (1983) Pain control. *Nursing Times* 27 April, p. 54; 4th May, p. 57. (A resumé of the nursing aspects of pain control.)

Ottoson, D. (1983) *The Physiology of the Nervous System*. Macmillan Press, Basingstoke.

Ross, J.S. and Wilson, K.J.W. (1987) *Anatomy and Physiology in Health and Illness* (6th edn). Churchill Livingstone, Edinburgh. (Particularly useful for its coverage of the anatomy of the nervous system.)

The development of   2
pain theories

Early civilisation perceived concepts such as the magical influence of spirits of the dead, or punishment for sins committed as some of the causes of pain.

Plato viewed pain as an 'affective' experience, that is an emotional experience, caused by a violent intrusion of elements into the body. He also considered the heart to be the centre of all sensation.

Aristotle agreed with Plato that the heart was the centre of all sensation, and did not include pain as one of the five classical senses which are: vision, hearing, taste, smell and touch, because he believed it to be the opposite affective experience to 'pleasure'. During this period, however, the term 'general sensation' was introduced to illustrate the diversity of the sensation, appreciating that pain can be felt in organs and tissues throughout the body, not just the skin.

In the 2nd century AD a Roman called Galen believed that it was the brain, not the heart, which was the centre for all sensation, and a specific set of nerves worked for each of the senses.

Several pain theories have been proposed since then with varying degrees of recognition. A background knowledge of the key pain theories that have evolved offers a deeper understanding and greater predictability when handling clinical diagnosis, treatment and patient care.

SPECIFICITY THEORY

The specificity theory is the traditional pain theory, and it proposes that a specific pain system carries messages from pain receptors in the skin to a pain centre in the brain.

The historical importance of the specificity theory should not be underestimated, and it is only relatively recently that more refined theories have been proposed showing it to have several obvious inadequacies.

9

Seventeenth century

In 1664 Descartes gave the first two classical descriptions of the specificity theory to illustrate his proposal that the pain system was a straight-through channel from the skin to the brain.

1. The system is like a bell-ringing mechanism in a church, i.e. a man pulls a rope at the bottom of the tower, and a bell rings in the belfry.
2. A flame sets particles in the foot into activity and the motion is transmitted up the leg and back into the head, where an alarm system is set off, i.e. the person feels pain and responds to it.

The classic illustration of this concept is shown in Fig.2.1

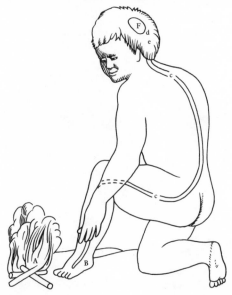

Fig. 2.1 Descartes' (1664) concept of the pain pathway. He writes: 'If for example fire (A) comes near the foot (B), the minute particles of this fire, which as you know move with great velocity, have the power to set in motion the spot of the skin of the foot which they touch, and by this means pulling upon the delicate thread (cc) which is attached to the spot of the skin, they open up at the same instant the pore (de) against which the delicate thread ends, just as by pulling at one end of a rope one makes to strike at the same instant a bell which hangs at the other end.'

Nineteenth century

Bell and Magendie were the first people to propose scientifically that it was exclusively sensory nerves which conveyed messages from the outside world to the brain. In 1842 Johannes Muller proposed the 'doctrine of specific nerve energies' in which special properties of sensory nerves determined the type of sensation they evoked.

Muller still recognised 'pain' as a variety of the classical mode of sensation 'touch'. However, he was unsure whether the quality of sensation was due to some specific energy, inherent in each of the sensory nerves themselves, or due to special properties in the brain centre where the nerves terminate.

Between 1894 and 1895, Max von Frey, a physician, published a series of articles which became the basis of the modern day specificity theory. In these articles he proposed that each major cutaneous modality, which are touch, cold, warmth and pain, had its own special projection system to the brain where it was interpreted in the centre responsible for the appropriate sensation. This differed from Muller who had still believed in a single sense of touch.

Von Frey also recognised that the skin was made up of a mosaic of four types of sensory spot. Following research into the distribution of specialised skin structures, he proposed that four of the identified structures were responsible for the four cutaneous modalities. Free nerve endings, for example, were identified as being responsible for pain.

Twentieth century

Von Frey's proposal that each cutaneous modality had its own type of specific nerve ending was extended to encompass peripheral nerves. A one-to-one relationship between receptor type, fibre size and quality of experience was recognised. This led to a theory proposing modality separation in peripheral nerves on the basis of fibre-diameter size, which is how the phrases 'A delta-fibre pain' and 'C fibre pain' became known.

More centrally, the ascending spinothalamic tract which is in the anterolateral part of the spinal cord was found to play a key role in pain sensation (Keele, 1957) and it became known as the 'pain pathway'.

Following proof that cortical lesions and excisions only rarely ablate pain, and sometimes even make it worse, it was proposed that the thalamus contains the pain centre, and the cortex may exert inhibitory control over it (Head, 1920).

All these proposals still presumed a straight-through pathway to a specific brain centre.

CONCLUSION

Although the specificity theory has many supporters, there have been a number of valid challenges on key aspects, some of which will be discussed in more detail in later theories.

Strong challenges have been made to the concept of four specific modalities matching with four specific receptors, with arguments against both the numbers and types of receptors involved.

The rigid, straight-through pain system, including the concept that the intensity of pain sensation is proportional to the stimulus, has been challenged with clinical evidence produced by causalgia, phantom limb pain and the neuralgias. Areas of the body totally unrelated to a primary pain problem have been known to become affected with pain. In addition, minimal touch, non-noxious stimulation—which is stimulation not capable of producing tissue damage—and unknown causes can produce intense pain for long periods of time.

It is also argued that pain is a subjective perception, that is, it is individual and can be modified by degrees of attention, emotional states and conditioning from past experiences. Examples of wounded soldiers in the war denying pain (Beecher, 1959), prove that intense noxious stimulation, which is stimulation potentially capable of producing tissue damage, can be prevented or modified.

PATTERN OR SUMMATION THEORY

Summation is the excitatory effects of converging inputs. Proposals were made by Goldscheider in 1898 which formed the basis of the pattern or summation theory. He proposed that the summation of the skin sensory input at the dorsal horn cells produced the particular patterns of nerve impulses that evoke pain.

When receptors normally activated by non-noxious heat or touch stimuli are subjected to excessive stimulations, or pathological conditions enhance the summation of impulses produced by normally non-noxious stimuli, pain occurs because the total output of cells exceeds a critical level. Abnormally long periods of summation would lead to chronic pain states or a delay period before an initial complaint is made.

Goldscheider also proposed that slowly conducting multi-synaptic fibre chains made up the 'spinal summation path' which transmitted pain to the brain.

Peripheral pattern theory

In 1955 Weddell and Sinclair proposed that pain was due to excessive peripheral stimulation of non-specific receptors, and the resultant patterns of nerve impulses were interpreted centrally as pain.

Spatial and temporal patterns of nerve impulses as opposed to modality specific transmission were thought to produce all cutaneous qualities. Spatial summation can occur when two weak stimuli deliver simultaneously to adjacent regions of the skin and give rise to sensation—singly, however, they would be unable to do so. Temporal summation can occur when a single stimulus to the skin is too weak to be perceived on its own, but gives rise to sensation if an identical stimulus occurs within a short time interval. The same fibre could at different times contribute towards the experience of touch, warmth, cold or pain.

The arguments against the peripheral pattern theory are that it proposes peripheral rather than central patterning, and all fibre endings are seen as alike which ignores physiological evidence of receptor-fibre specialisation.

Central summation theory

In 1943 Livingstone made the first proposal that a central neural mechanism is responsible for pain syndromes such as phantom limb pain, causalgia and the neuralgias. He proposed that:

1. Pathological stimulation of nerves, for example after peripheral nerve injury, initiates activity in reverberatory circuits (closed,

self-exciting loops of neurons) in the dorsal horns in the spinal cord.

2. Central interpretation of pain is produced when volleys of impulses are transmitted from the dorsal horns to the brain.

3. The reverberatory activity in the dorsal horns can spread to the lateral and ventral horns in the spinal cord, activating the autonomic and motor systems which produce, for example, sweating and jerking movements and other manifestations. More abnormal input is then produced and creates a vicious circle between the central and peripheral processes which allows abnormal spinal cord activity to continue.

4. Anxiety and fear triggered off by pain can also be fed from the brain into the reverberatory circuits, helping to continue abnormal activity.

Fig.2.2 illustrates the concept of central summation

The major argument against this theory is seen in clinical evidence: when surgical lesions of the spinal cord are performed, for example bilateral cordotomy, in the majority of cases they do not abolish pain for any length of time. This indicates that there must be mechanisms at a higher level than the dorsal horns.

Sensory interaction theory

The sensory interaction theory is related to the central summation theory, and it provided valuable new concepts which were considered as the gate control theory evolved (see Chapter 3).

The theory proposes that summation of slowly conducting pain fibres can be inhibited by a specialised input control system of more rapidly conducting fibres. If the inhibitory fibres were not allowed to work, then pathological pain states could occur.

In 1959 Noordenbus proposed that the small fibres were those responsible for carrying pain, and the large fibres were the inhibitory control system. Should the small fibres become more dominant than the large fibres, then pathological pain states could occur.

Noordenbus also proposed that a more diffuse multi-synaptic system as opposed to the straight-through system in the spinal cord may provide the answer to the problem of why pain is still seen following surgical lesions such as cordotomy.

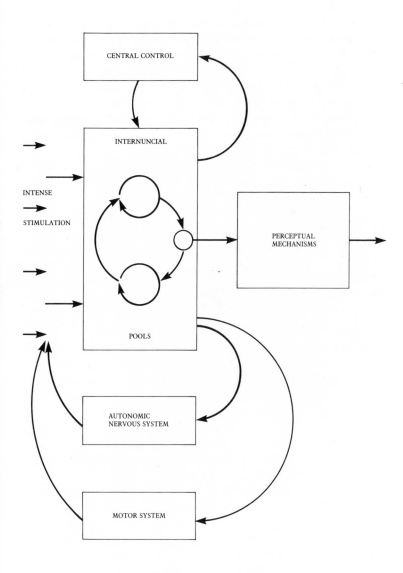

Fig. 2.2 Central summation theory – a schematic diagram.

REFERENCES

Beecher, H. K. (1959) *Measurement of Subjective Responses*. Oxford University Press, New York.

Bishop, G. H. (1946) Neural mechanisms of cutaneous sense. *Physiological Review* **26**, 77–102.

Frey, M. von (1895) Beitrage zur Sinnesphysiologie der Haut. *Ber. d Kgl. Sachs. Ges. D. Wiss. Math. Phys. KL.*, **47**, 166–84.

Goldscheider, A. (1894) *Ueber den Schmerz in physiologischer und klinischer Hinsicht*. Hirschwald, Berlin.

Head, H. (1920) *Studies in Neurology*. Kegan Paul, London.

Keele, K. D. (1957) *Anatomies of Pain*. Oxford University Press, London.

Livingstone, W. K. (1943) *Pain Mechanisms*. Macmillan, New York.

Muller, J. (1842) *Elements of Physiology*. Taylor, London.

Noordenbus, W. (1959) *Pain*. Elsevier, Amsterdam.

Rose, J. E. and Mountcastle, V. B. (1959) Touch and kinethesis. *Handbook of Physiology*. Vol. I pp. 387–429.

Sinclair, D. C. (1967) *Cutaneous Sensation*. Oxford University Press, London.

Weddell, G. (1955) Synthesis and the chemical senses. *Annual Review of Psychology* **6**, 119–36.

BIBLIOGRAPHY

Melzack, R. and Wall, P. D. (1989) *The Challenge of Pain*. Penguin, Harmondsworth.

The gate control theory   3

In 1965 Melzack and Wall proposed the gate control theory of pain which offered answers to many of the deficiencies recognised in earlier theories. The theory is based on five proposals:

PROPOSAL 1

A spinal gating mechanism exists in the dorsal horns of the spinal cord. This modulates the conduction of nerve impulses from afferent fibres to spinal cord transmission cells.

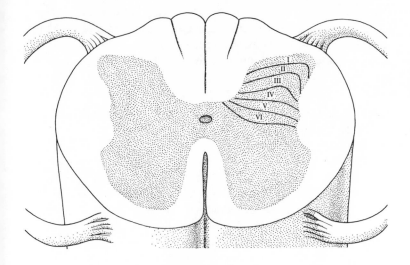

Fig. 3.1 The six laminae of the dorsal horn. I–III contains the substantia gelatinosa; V contains the spinal transmission cells

The dorsal horn consists of six layers, or 'laminae' (see Fig.3.1) and the proposal is based on evidence that:

1. The substantia gelatinosa within laminae I–III consists of a highly specialised closed system of cells throughout the length of the spinal cord on both sides. It also receives large and small fibres from afferent nerves, and is able to influence the activity of cells that project to the brain.
2. The spinal transmission cells in lamina V are thought to be those most likely to be involved in pain perception and response because:
   (a) They receive input from small afferent fibres from skin, muscle and viscera;
   (b) Activity is influenced by fibres descending from the brain;
   (c) Response is made to a wide range of stimulus activities;
   (d) Output is influenced by relative activity in large and small fibres.

PROPOSAL 2

Patterned information such as pressure, temperature, and chemical changes are transmitted from specialised receptor-fibre units in the skin to the dorsal horns via sensory nerves. When these spatial and temporal patterns of nerve impulses arrive at the dorsal horn two effects are seen:

1. The spinal transmission cells are excited and project information to the brain.
   (a) Large fibre activity has been found to produce inhibition of transmission, that is to say 'closes the gate'.
   (b) Small fibre activity has been found to facilitate transmission, that is to say 'opens the gate'. This provides the basis for summation, prolonged activity and spread of pain to other areas of the body. Activity can, however, be modulated by other activities within the nervous system.
2. The substantia gelatinosa is activated as a 'gate', influencing the transmission of impulses from afferent fibre terminals to spinal cord cells. The amount of information sent to the brain by the transmission cells is therefore modulated.

It is thought that this was largely due to the cells of the substantia gelatinosa acting directly on the pre-synaptic axon terminals. This would block the impulses in the terminals, or decrease the amount of transmitter substance they released. Evidence of post-synaptic action on the spinal transmission cells was not available in 1965, but it was thought this may also be involved in the 'gating' mechanism.

PROPOSAL 3

Reticular formation within the brain stem is made up of diffuse, interconnecting nerve fibres that are spread out between bundles of passing fibre tracts which either descend back down into the spinal cord, or extend directly or indirectly to most areas in the cerebrum (see Fig.3.2).

Descending efferent fibres from the brain stem reticular formation, in particular the mid-brain reticular areas, influence pain processes in the dorsal horns because they are thought to exert inhibitory control over activity in the spinal transmission cells in lamina V.

These descending efferent fibres make up the reticulo-spinal projection system, and can be influenced by other factors such as:

1. Somatic projections from all areas of the body, including sight and hearing, are present in reticular formation. These are able to exert a modulating influence on transmission through the dorsal horns.
2. Fibres from the cortex, in particular the frontal cortex project to the reticular formation. Transmission can therefore be modulated by cognitive processes such as past experiences.

PROPOSAL 4

The dorsal column carries many of the large nerve fibres from the sensory root at which they enter the spinal cord, to the brain. Large, rapidly conducting cortico-spinal fibres are also thought to be present in the dorsal column projection system and these make up the 'central control trigger' mechanism.

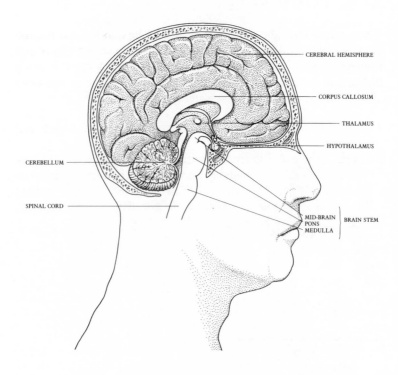

Fig. 3.2   The position of the reticular formation. The reticular formation is present within the brain stem, and has connections down into the spinal cord and upwards to more central areas.

This mechanism allows cognitive processes such as past experiences to influence responses to body signals by identifying, evaluating and localising them rapidly.

One area to which these rapidly conducting fibres project is the dorsal horns, therefore pain perception and response can be inhibited by cognitive processes before the system is activated.

PROPOSAL 5

When output from the transmission cells in the dorsal horns reaches or exceeds a critical level, the 'action system' for pain experience and response is activated. When this takes place sensory input is being filtered and continuing sensory and affective activity occurs at a series of levels in the central nervous system, for example:

1. Interaction occurs between the gate control system and the action system.
2. The brain may influence resetting of the gate control system several times as it analyses and acts on the sensory input it receives. When Melzack and Wall proposed the gate control theory they illustrated it with a schematic diagram which encompassed their five proposals (see Fig.3.3).

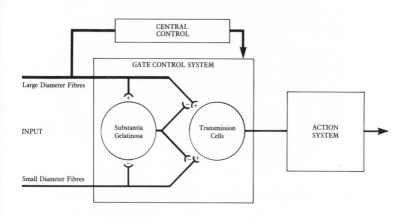

Fig. 3.3 Gate control theory – Mark 1. Reprinted with permission. Copyright 1965 by the AAAS.

FURTHER PROPOSALS

The gate control theory of 1965 is continually being reviewed and updated as greater knowledge is gained of the systems involved, such as:

1. Inhibitory and excitatory links within the substantia gelatinosa have been highlighted (see Proposal 2). For example, peptides such as substance P which are released from nerve terminals and act on nerve cells have been found to be present in the small diameter nerve fibres, in particular the C fibres. The exact role of these substances is still not entirely clear, but their levels have been found to be reduced in the spinal cord efferent terminals within the substantia gelatinosa following nerve injury.

2. Evidence of post-synaptic action in addition to pre-synaptic action has been found (see Proposal 2).

3. Further importance has been placed on the part the brain stem inhibitory system plays after sensory input has left the transmission cells in the gate, and its resultant feedback into the dorsal horns (see Proposal 3).

An updated diagram of the gate control theory encompassing these proposals was compiled by Melzack and Wall (see Fig.3.4).

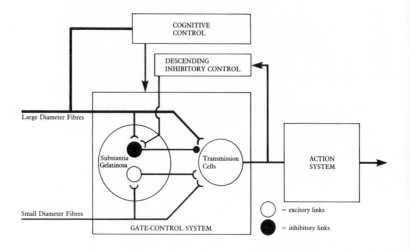

Fig. 3.4   Gate control theory — Mark 2.

CONCLUSION

The whole process of piecing together the mechanisms involved in pain and its resultant activities is extremely complex, but nevertheless fascinating. It is an ever-changing situation, and research is now encompassing not only further advances in the gate control mechanism but also other ideas such as the role of endorphins and chemical transmitters, and how psychological factors influence pain. Some of these topics will be discussed as appropriate in conjunction with other topics.

Whatever breakthroughs are being made within the field of pain research, it is abundantly clear that the more knowledge we have about pain, the more we still have to learn.

BIBLIOGRAPHY

Gibson, J. (1974) *A Guide to the Nervous System.* Faber and Faber, London.

Latham, J. (1985) Functional anatomy and physiology of pain. *The Professional Nurse,* 1, 2, 42–44.

Melzack, R. and Wall, P.D. (1965) Pain mechanisms: a new theory. *Science,* 150, 971–979.

Melzack, R. and Wall, P.D. (1989) *The Challenge of Pain.* Penguin, Harmondsworth.

Ottoson, D. (1983) *The Physiology of the Nervous System.* Macmillan Press, Basingstoke.

Ross, J.S. and Wilson, K.J.W. (1987) *Anatomy and Physiology in Health and Illness* (6th edn). Churchill Livingstone, Edinburgh.

Wall, P.D. and Melzack, R. (1989) *Textbook of Pain* (2nd edn). Churchill Livingstone, Edinburgh.

Assessment, measurement
and observation of pain   4

Effective treatment of pain is not possible until an accurate assessment has been made of the problem. However, pain is extremely difficult to assess objectively as each person perceives, describes and reacts to pain differently. Assessment therefore requires not only in-depth history taking but also accurate measurement and continuous observation. The initial assessment should be used as a base line for comparison with further assessments, measurements and observations.

Having gained a basic knowledge of how to assess a patient in pain this can be adapted to many different situations, for example patients undergoing surgery, patients with chronic pain, the elderly, children and the handicapped.

ASSESSMENT OF A PAIN HISTORY

Physical, psychological, social and environmental factors can all influence the way in which a patient in pain presents. Each of these factors should therefore be assessed as accurately as possible to try and ascertain what part each factor plays in the perception of pain. Has the physical pain, for example, caused any psychological or social problems or have any social or psychological problems perhaps initiated or exacerbated the physical problems? There is often an overlap on these two essential questions but whatever the primary cause of the pain it is a very real problem and should be treated as such.

PHYSICAL ASPECTS

Initial onset of pain

It is important to compare the medical history with the patient's own idea of what caused the pain so that similarities and discrepancies

24

can be evaluated. The patient may, for example, think that an event totally unrelated to the actual clinical cause was responsible for the pain, and this may affect the way in which future treatment is managed.

The initial onset of pain can be attributed to events such as trauma, illness, surgery or an apparently unknown cause.

Anatomical position of the pain

The area or areas of the body which are causing the pain can be most effectively recorded by illustrating the sites on a diagram of the body. This chart can be filled in by either the patient or the assessor, and can be used to analyse the primary and referred sites of the pain.

Copies of the same chart can be used throughout the course of treatment so that any changes can be accurately compared and evaluated.

Description of the pain

A clinically useful description of pain by a patient can often be difficult to obtain because of pain being an individual, subjective experience. However, patients should be encouraged to describe their pain as key words and phrases can often suggest the type of pain involved, for example, 'burning' indicates nerve involvement, 'dull ache' indicates visceral pain and 'recurring or intermittent' or 'continuous' indicates the pattern of the pain.

Questionnaires such as 'The McGill Pain Questionnaire' (Melzack, 1975) can be useful in gaining a more objective appreciation of the patient's description. This will be discussed in more detail in Chapter 5.

Factors affecting pain

Factors affecting the pain should be noted, for example, time of day, activity, position, food, stress, anxiety and isolation.

Although the patient will be asked directly what makes the pain better or worse, the assessor should listen for other factors throughout the assessment which the patient may not think important. Thus, the patient and the assessor may sometimes conclude that different factors affect the pain.

Previous treatment

The management and effectiveness of previous treatments should be recorded so that a practical plan of care can be formulated. If some treatments have been tried in the past it may be inappropriate to try them again. Should a patient have bad memories of a previous treatment, it would be unwise to offer this treatment as a first option even if it may be felt to be potentially the most effective. This is because there may be less patient compliance at the beginning of treatment when no time has been allowed to build up a trusting relationship between the patient and the caring team.

It is also important to document the finer details of previous treatments because different management of the same treatment may be possible. Examples of this include the anatomical placement of electrode pads for transcutaneous nerve stimulation and the regimes used for medication.

Other medical history

Any other medical history thought to be relevant by either the assessor or the patient should be documented for reference.

PSYCHOLOGICAL ASPECTS

Following the assessment of a patient's physical pain it may be felt that a more in-depth psychological assessment may be needed of certain points which were picked up in the course of assessment. These may include the possibility of obsessive personality, stress, tension and changes in life style which may indicate problems such as depression or behavioural disorders.

Both subjective and objective assessments of how the patient feels are useful and will be discussed in Chapter 5.

The key role of the nurse is to recognise when a patient is in need of more specialist help and to expedite an appropriate referral.

SOCIAL AND ENVIRONMENTAL ASPECTS

To be in a position to offer practical and effective answers to a patient's pain problem, social and environmental factors surrounding the patient should be assessed. These factors are an important consideration when deciding on the most appropriate treatment for a patient. They may also influence, either positively or negatively, the potential response to any treatment.

The family

Various situations involving the patient and his family and friends can influence the pain itself and reactions to treatment, for example:

1. The family may be very supportive to both the patient and the caring team, thus allowing every chance of active treatment and positive response to that treatment.
2. The pain may be providing the patient with secondary gain such as extra attention from family and friends which would not be available in normal circumstances.
3. The patient may relate most closely to a friend, but is not able to see that person so frequently because they are not 'family'. This may include groups such as homosexuals and lesbians.
4. A patient in hospital may worry about a dependent at home.
5. Marital problems between a patient and his spouse may exacerbate or change a pain syndrome.
6. Bereavement could be causing loneliness or depression.

Housing and environment

Situations associated with both housing and environment can influence the way people cope with pain, examples of these include:

1. If the patient lives alone, or shares with other members of the family or friends.
2. Whether the housing is well-maintained, or is in need of repair or up-grading.
3. The area in which the housing is situated, a quiet residential area or a 'problem estate'.
4. Changes in the home situation over the relevant period of time, for example, a move from one house area to another.

Work status

It is important to assess the patient's work status as this can often influence or be influenced by a pain problem. Factors that should be looked into include:

1. The type of employment the patient is involved in.
2. If the patient is unemployed, how long this has been a problem.
3. Any change or loss of job during the relevant period. If this was so, it should be known whether this occurred before the pain presented, or as a result of the pain.
4. If the patient has retired, when this occurred and any implications the patient feels this may have had.

Hobbies

Interests and hobbies should be discussed with the patient as these may have changed during the time the pain has been present. These facts can often be useful when starting to rebuild the patient's life constructively in conjunction with other appropriate treatments.

OBSERVATION AND MEASUREMENT

Informal observation

It is in the situation where the patient is unaware of being observed that the most natural reactions are seen. It is therefore extremely useful when observing the patient in pain to learn the art of being able to do so informally in addition to more formal situations.

The most important observations to note when the patient is alone or interacting with relatives, doctors, nurses or other patients are:

1. Physical movement, e.g. mobility, positional changes, or restriction of movement.
2. Facial expressions, e.g. relaxed or screwed up with pain.
3. Mood, e.g. depressed, stoical or happy.

Interaction with different groups may give rise to different reactions such as reacting 'normally' for their complaint with a nurse, putting on a stoical non-complaining attitude with a doctor, and making the most of the situation in front of relatives.

Formal observation and measurement

Although informal observation of pain can be informative it is important to make use of formal observations and measurements. Formal documentation encourages more continuity of care and accurate assessment which can often be difficult with the inevitable problem of changes of staff throughout each day.

1. There are several charts available to measure pain, some of which can be rather complicated and misleading to the patient. One of the most popular measurement charts is the Visual Analogue Scale (VAS) (Fig.4.1). The patient marks on the line the intensity of pain between 'No Pain' and 'Worst Pain Imaginable'. Another measurement chart is the Intensity Rating Scale (IRS), which gives descriptions of pain. The patient marks the description that he/she would use to describe the pain (Fig. 4.2). Any scoring scale should not be included on a sheet with other scales, writing or drawings as these may consciously or subconsciously catch the patient's attention and therefore possibly bias a more objective assessment.

No pain   Worst pain
                                     imaginable

Fig. 4.1 Visual Analogue Scale. Mark on the line the severity of your pain at the moment.

2. Mechanical pain recorders, whereby the patient presses a button at regular intervals throughout the 24 hour period, are a useful method of pain measurement. The more firmly the patient presses, the more intense is the pain. Should the patient be asleep then no pain is recorded.

   The pain recorder is useful for research purposes because it allows a continuous 24 hour period of assessment which one person would find difficult to cover. In research more than one person assessing a patient in pain leads to questions about subjectivity of assessment.

3. For outpatients, pain diaries are a useful way of combining measurements with the patient's description of the pain. This should include comments on how the pain may have changed and how, if at all, it has affected their life. The most accurate assessment can be gained if the patient fills the diary in at the same time each day.

Fig. 4.2   Intensity Rating Scale.

4. A nursing pain assessment chart can be adapted to the individual needs of each clinical unit. This leads to more specific nursing care plans and therefore more effective care for the patient in pain. Fig. 4.3 illustrates an example of such a chart.

ADAPTION OF ASSESSMENT, MEASUREMENT AND OBSERVATION OF PAIN

Surgical patients

The requirements of a pain observation chart for surgical patients are usually more frequent observations over a limited period of time. It has been argued that by introducing a pain assessment chart pre-operatively, despite the fact that it may initially appear to

(continues on p. 34)

CAMBERWELL HEALTH AUTHORITY

PAIN ASSESSMENT CHART

TO BE COMPLETED BY NURSE AND PATIENT WHENEVER POSSIBLE

1. **WHERE IS THE PAIN?**

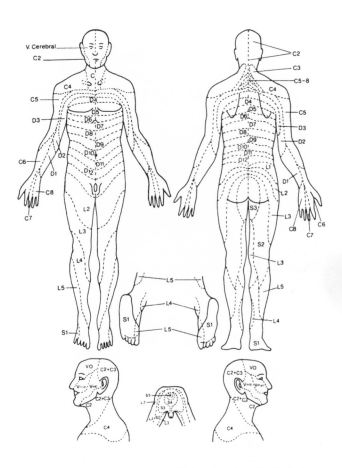

Fig. 4.3   Pain Assessment Chart. King's College Hospital Pain Relief Unit.

2.   **TIME AND DURATION OF PAIN** – Tick where applicable

Recurring pain, lasting a few minutes	
Pain lasting for several hours	
Pain constant, no relief	

Approximately how often do you get pain in a day?

3.   **HOW WOULD YOU DESCRIBE YOUR PAIN?**

4.   **NURSING CARE PLAN FOR PAIN RELIEF**

PROBLEM	ACTION TO BE TAKEN e.g. Analgesia, position change, counselling

PAIN ASSESSMENT CHART – NURSING CARE CONTINUATION SHEET

To be completed by nurse and patient whenever possible.

DATE AND TIME	SITE OF PAIN	DESCRIPTION OF PAIN	V.A.S. SCORE	I.R. SCORE	ACTION TAKEN	RESULT OF ACTION AND FOLLOW-UP

heighten anticipation and fear of pain, during the post-operative period better pain management may be achieved because the patient has been counselled about what may happen, there is no fear of the unknown, and the pain is often not so severe as the patient anticipates (Hasking and Welchen, 1985).

Patients with chronic pain

This group of patients should be managed as much as possible on an outpatient basis to maintain as normal a life style as possible. For this reason the use of pain diaries in combination with accurate clinic assessment is an important part of their management.

The handicapped

The degree of disability, either physical or mental, should be ascertained from the patient or key carers as appropriate. An assessment should then be made utilising the most effective forms of communication available to the patient such as body and sign language, drawings and special machines adapted for the patient.

The elderly

It can be difficult to assess the elderly because of communication problems due to failing sight, hearing or mental faculties. These factors should always be taken into account when deciding on the most appropriate method of assessment. It is also useful to include the person who is most closely associated with the patient such as a member of the family or a carer, so that a more accurate assessment of the pain can be made.

Children

It is particularly difficult to accurately assess a child's pain. Areas that need special investigation prior to deciding the most appropriate form of assessment include:

1. The developmental stage of the child, including factors such as verbal and social communication.

2. Previous experiences of pain and the child's reaction to them.
3. The family and environmental situation.

An example of a pain assessment chart developed for children is the Eland Color Tool (Eland, 1985) (Fig.4.4). Instructions for its use are also outlined with the chart.

Designed for use during an interview, the Eland Color Tool lets the child show you what hurts and how much. In addition to its value during assessment, this tool can provide early diagnostic clues to disease.

To use the Eland Color Tool, obtain a set of crayons and body outlines. (Copy the body outlines reproduced here for use during the interview.) Then follow these steps.

- Ask the child. 'What kinds of things have hurt you before?'
- If he doesn't answer, ask 'Has anyone ever stuck your finger for blood? What did that feel like?'
- After discussing several things that have hurt the child in the past, ask 'Of all the things that have ever hurt you, what was the worst?'
- Give the child eight crayons and ask him 'Of these colours which is like the thing that hurts you the most?' Important: Name the painful incident specifically.
- Place the crayon representing severe pain to one side.
- Ask 'Which colour is like a hurt, but not as bad as your worst hurt?' (Again, specifically name the hurt.)
- Place the second crayon next to the one representing severe pain.
- Continue in this way, choosing crayons that represent just a little hurt and no hurt at all.
- Give the four chosen crayons to the child along with the body outlines. You might write the child's name above or below the outline.
- Ask the child to use his crayons to show you on the outline where he hurts a lot, a middle amount, just a little, or not at all.
- Ask, 'Is this hurt happening right now, or is it from earlier today? Does it happen all the time or on and off?'
- Remember to include a colour key on the tool.
- Document all the child's responses, using his own words.

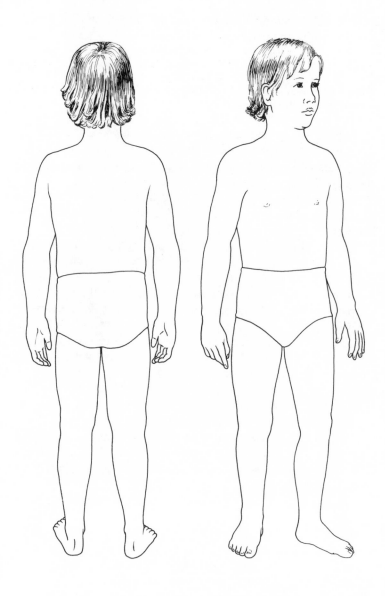

Fig.4.4 The Eland Color Tool. Reprinted with permission from Nursing Now **Pain**, Springhouse Corporation.

REFERENCES

Eland, J. (1985) *Nursing New Series, Pain.* Springhouse Corporation, pp. 108–119.

Hasking, J. and Welchen, E. (1985) *Post-operative pain: Understanding its Nature and How to Treat it.* Faber and Faber, London, pp. 73–150.

Melzack, R. (1975) The McGill Pain Questionnaire major properties and scoring methods. *Pain*, 1, 275–99.

BIBLIOGRAPHY

Melzack, R. (1985) (ed) *Pain Measurement and Assessment.* Raven Press, New York.

Raiman, J.A. (1982) Responding to pain. *Nursing.* November, 1362.

Pain and the person   5

by Maureen Williams
Principal Clinical Psychologist
Pain Relief Unit
King's College Hospital, London

Nurses in their training learn a great deal about the anatomy and physiology of 'pain pathways' and the pharmacology of analgesics, but often little information is given about the psychological and social factors which influence the experience of pain. Pain can be viewed as an emotional communication on the part of the patient and it is nurses who spend by far the greatest amount of time with patients and get to know and understand patients in face to face contact with them. Therefore it is essential for the nurse to understand what is being communicated by the patient and to realise the full repertoire of skills that can be brought to bear in helping the patient handle pain. Prolonged pain can make an individual feel out of control which in turn leads to anxiety and panic. Good nursing can reduce the patient's tension and anxiety which in turn dissipates panic and increases the patient's tolerance of pain, the patient then feels more comfortable and once again more in control of himself.

INDIVIDUAL COPING STYLES: PERSONALITY VARIABLES WHICH INFLUENCE PAIN REACTIONS

Personality is a much misused word. We speak of people having 'lots of personality' or 'no personality' when what we mean is that we do or do not like their particular personality. Personality as defined by psychologists is a term used to describe those aspects of the entire range of an individual's behaviour which are persistent and enduring. It is behaviour which is mentioned in this definition because it is that aspect which can be seen and even measured by others, but the behaviour is the end product of the complex interaction between the affective, i.e. emotional, behavioural and cognitive aspects of the person illustrated in Fig.5.1.

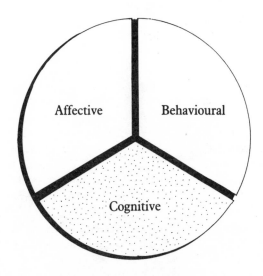

Fig. 5.1 Complex interaction between the affective, behavioural and cognitive aspects of the person.

Personality is only fully developed in adulthood. Babies are not born with their personalities completely formed although doting mothers would disagree, instead personality develops as the child grows. Initially the baby feels part of the mother and it is through the mother's handling of the child that it develops an awareness of the limits of its own body, i.e. body image. Then with the mother's verbal interactions with the child, the child starts to develop an image of itself, i.e. self-image, when the feedback received is positive the child develops a sense of self-esteem (Fig.5.2).

It is important to understand this development and to realise that pain and illness can disturb and distort the person's body image, their self-image and their self-esteem (a clear example of this is in post-mastectomy patients who say the feel like 'lepers' and no longer feel feminine) leading to a very deep level of emotional pain (Fig.5.3).

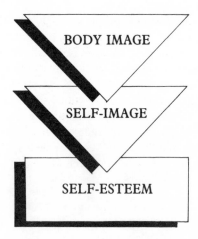

Fig. 5.2   Shows the progression from body image to self-esteem.

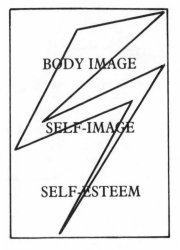

Fig. 5.3   One or all of these can be distorted by pain.

Simultaneously with the development of the personality and sense of personal identity the child is subjected to social, religious, ethnic, cultural and environmental influences. Patterns of behaviour are modelled by significant adults for the child and this includes pain behaviour. Parental attitudes to illness can differ greatly. Some parents reinforce illness behaviour and only give the child attention when ill and others become over-anxious themselves and thereby panic the child. The experience of early hospitalisation also can be significant, although considerable strides have been made in recent years to make a child's stay in hospital far less traumatic than previously.

Nurses also have their own individual personalities and bring to their work their own learned attitudes to pain and illness behaviour. A very clear example of the attitude of nurses affecting treatment is given in Michael Bond's (1979) book (Table 5.1). It can be seen that there is a complex interaction between nurse and patient.

Table 5.1 The pattern of administration of analgesic drugs to men and women in radiotherapy wards. Drugs requested and given during one week (Bond, 1979).

	Men	Women
Number of patients	15	12
Number of occasions drugs given at patient's request	23	28
Number of occasions drugs given on initiative of nurses	1	22
Number of occasions on which nurses refused patient's request for analgesic drugs	18	0

Affective

Firstly let us look at the effective aspect. With acute pain anxiety is high and this anxiety can lead to hypervigilance whereby the patient makes a closer examination of bodily sensations and by focusing on them magnifies them, further increasing the patient's anxiety. While there is an increase in somatisation and hypochondriasis the patient is not usually depressed as he hopes for a full recovery.

With chronic pain, depression is often more predominant than anxiety, although anxiety too may be present. The patient has fears and worries about the pain and suffers from anticipatory anxiety, e.g. has a fear that the pain will become intolerable at some point in the future. This can make patients tense and reduce their tolerance to the pain they are currently experiencing and it is known that depression can actually amplify the pain felt. The patients start to feel helpless and hopeless, this increases the patients' passivity and thereby decreases their desire for active cooperation in any treatment and any chance of a treatment alliance is lost.

Behavioural

On a behavioural level the pain and illness behaviours which were learned in childhood lead the patient to consult a physician, take medication and alter their life style in order to adjust to the discomfort they are feeling. Often patients fall into one of the two major categories.

Complainers   Those who clearly manifest their distress: they may be extroverts, or patients who show histrionic, hysterical or hypochondriacal behaviour. These patients can be very difficult to empathise with but it is this that they need and not the sympathy which they are demanding.

Non-complainers   They do not necessarily experience less pain, but if they have phobic or anxious personalities, are stoical, introverted or severely depressed they may find it difficult to express the pain they are feeling and thereby gain the reassurance and attention that they need. A good nurse can listen with a 'third ear' and put their pain into words for them and ensure that they get the analgesia that they need.

Cognitive

On a cognitive level, the patients' perception of their pain is important, what does it mean to them? Does it mean that their life is threatened or that they are very seriously ill? Are they thinking in a very n̲ ̲ ̲ ̲ way, for example telling themselves that there is no ̲ ̲ ̲ ̲ self-esteem seriously affected because they have lost ̲ ̲ ̲ ̲ ̲eir job, or their status or position in the family since ̲ ̲ ̲ ̲ ̲ger be the breadwinner? Also it should be remem- ̲ ̲ ̲ ̲ ̲: can talk themselves into real pain and this can have ̲ ̲ ̲ ̲ ̲e patient, they are known as secondary gains.

Secondary gains

Pain can often provide an opportunity to 'opt out' while at the same time allowing the patient the pleasure of feeling a martyr, while discharging hostile impulses in a concealed and indirect way towards relatives and doctors. Pain behaviour can be used to elicit social support, to obtain drugs, to express anger, to avoid intimacy, to control key relatives and others, to avoid anxiety-provoking situation, to obtain compensation, to gain early retirement on medical grounds, to avoid undesired social, vocational or family responsibilities. The motivation may be conscious or unconscious. At a conscious level patients may be seeking financial gain or at an unconscious level a conversion reaction may occur when patients refuse to admit that, apart from the pain, they have any problems in their life. In either case the end result is being able to exploit the advantages of being cared for.

In some patients there can be a sinister dynamic in which the patient gets some masochistic pleasure from the pain and sees himself as the 'victim' while at the same time gaining some sadistic pleasure from punishing his family with his pain behaviour. Fortunately, there are not many such patients (Table 5.2).

Table 5.2 Pain can be used by patients in a manipulative way to:

Elicit social support
Control key relatives
Avoid intimacy
Express anger
Avoid anxiety-provoking situations

ASSESSMENT OF PERSONALITY AND PAIN

Personality

It is important to assess the patients' personality, their attitude to pain and their motivation accurately.

Questionnaires are simple to administer and score and easy for the patient to complete. The Minnesota Multiphasic Personality Inventory is very widely used in America but as it is extremely long it takes a very fit patient to complete it. In England the Eysenck Personality Questionnaire (Eysenck and Eysenck, 1975) is more popular, but a better measure of the personalities of pain patients is probably obtained with 'The Middlesex Hospital Questionnaire' (Crown and Crisp, 1966). This consists of 48 questions which highlight six different personality traits: free-floating anxiety, phobic anxiety, depression, hysteria, somatic complaints and obsessionality. It can be used to draw up a personality profile of the patient, used as a screen for psychoneurotic traits or for measuring change before and after treatment. Research carried out in our pain clinic shows that there are marked differences in scores between pain patients and those of a normal population and those of a psychiatric population (Table 5.3).

Where there is evidence of a psychiatric condition the Beck Depression Inventory or Zigmond and Snaith's (1983) Hospital Anxiety and Depression Scale can be administered.

There are questionnaires which can test for hostility for example Snaith's Irritability Scale (Snaith *et al*, 1978) or Spielberger's Self-Analysis Questionnaire (Spielberger *et al*, 1982).

There are also measures of stressful life events. These can help to explain why a patient presents with pain at a particular time in his life, even though the pain has been long-standing. For example grief due to the loss of a loved one can increase the emotional pain felt by a patient but he communicates this as an increase of his physical pain level.

Pain

Pain is a complex experience but it can be measured accurately. One measures it clinically: to aid in diagnosis and decide on the appropriate treatment; to monitor fluctuations in pain levels during treatment; to evaluate treatment efficacy and for reliable monitoring of pain over time.

Table 5.3 Examples of questions from the Middlesex Hospital Questionnaire. (From *Crown-Crisp Experimental Index*, published by Hodder and Stoughton.)

Question	Response		
Do you often feel upset for no obvious reason?		Yes	No
Do people ever say that you are too conscientious?		Yes	No
Do you enjoy being the centre of attention?		Yes	No
Do you feel that life is too much effort?	At times	Often	Never
Do you sometimes feel tingling or pricking sensations in your body, arms, or legs?	Rarely	Frequently	Never

No pain	Worst pain imaginable

Mark on this line the severity of your pain at this moment.

Fig. 5.4 Visual Analogue Scale is a popular and simple method for the patient to use to measure his pain.

One can listen to the patient's verbal report of the pain or one can use rating scales. There can be verbal ones (adjectival) or numerical or visual analogue scales (Fig.5.4). The Visual Analogue Scale is a popular and simple method for the patient to use to measure his pain. Questionnaires describe pain, for example The McGill Pain Questionnaire (Melzack, 1975) explores the sensory, affective and evaluative dimensions of pain (Fig. 5.5). As some of the vocabulary used is complex and the questionnaire rather long for a very ill patient to complete, Melzack devised a shorter version in 1987 which uses only

15 pain descriptors. The new questionnaire retains a present pain intensity rating scale and includes a visual analogue scale.

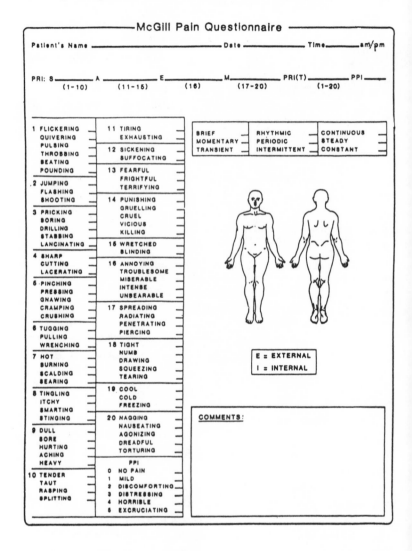

Fig. 5.5 The McGill Pain Questionnaire.

Pain diaries, a form of self-monitoring, can be an accurate tool, because when kept daily they are less subject to distortions of memory.

Behavioural assessments can be used for pain behaviour to:
1. Measure somatic interventions, e.g. taking medication, seeking surgery or nerve blocks.
2. Measure impaired functioning, e.g. reduced mobility or range of movement, avoidance of occupational commitments or impaired interpersonal relationships.
3. Measure pain complaints, e.g. moaning, contortions or facial expressions.

Illness Behaviour questionnaires such as the one devised by Pilowsky and Spence (1975) look at the patient's attitude to his illness. Some sample questions from this questionnaire are:
- Are you upset by the way people take your illness?
- Do you frequently try to explain to others how you are feeling?
- Do you find your illness affects your sexual relations?
- Would all your worries be over if you were physically healthy?
- Are you more sensitive to pain than other people?
- Do you think there is something seriously wrong with your body?

Fourteen items taken from the original 52 item questionnaire form the 'Whiteley Index' and these items have been shown to be able to discriminate between hypochondriacal and non-hypochondriacal patients.

There may be occasions when you feel that more specialised help is needed, for instance, from a psychiatrist, a psychologist or a social worker and the nurse should feel free to suggest that such help should be sought. Specialised help for pain patients can include:

Psychotherapy
Behaviour therapy
Cognitive therapy
Assertion training
Vocational guidance
Grief therapy

Marital therapy
Family therapy
Referral to a psychosexual clinic
Referral to an infertility clinic
Advice re litigation

TREATMENT

What can be done for the patient in pain when the pain and the feeling of loss of control become predominant and everything else sinks into the background? The nurse can be the best monitor of the level of analgesia required and can offer the patient reassurance that he will not be allowed to suffer unnecessarily. There are also many techniques which can be employed to reduce the pain effectively and some of them are quite simple (Table 5.4).

Table 5.4 Psychological approaches to pain control (Tan, 1982)

Relaxation techniques

Hypnosis

Modification of pain behaviours

Modelling

Biofeedback procedures

Provision of preparatory information

Cognitive coping skills or strategies for { 'Avoiders' 'Copers'

Using distraction or attention diversion techniques

(a) Imaginative inattention

(b) Imaginative transformation of pain

(c) Imaginative transformation of context

(d) Attention-diversion (external)

(e) Attention-diversion (internal)

(f) Somatisation

Relaxation techniques work well since anxiety and relaxation cannot coexist. If because of physical damage full muscular relaxation cannot be obtained simple breathing exercises can be used. Such deep levels of relaxation can be reached by most patients that it borders on hypnosis. The level of relaxation experienced can be greatly increased by the use of relaxing images. Suggestion can also be used, whereby one suggests to the patient that the pain is lessening in intensity and that tolerance to it is under the patient's control.

Modelling has proven particularly useful with children, for example, when they have been shown a film of other children undergoing the same surgical procedure that they are to have, their anxiety is shown to be markedly reduced. With adult patients suitable 'models' for more appropriate behaviour can often be found on the same ward as the patient and these should be used.

In general it is useful to provide information, preparation and education for the patient about forthcoming procedures, for example surgery or a painful dressing so that the patient has some way of knowing what is about to occur and thereby the level of anticipatory anxiety is reduced. Not every patient responds well to prior information. 'Avoiders' (those who use denial as a defence) respond poorly but 'copers' benefit from the information, so again accurate assessment of your patient is essential.

One can modify pain behaviour by ignoring that behaviour, for example with attention-seeking, dependent-type illness behaviour (wincing, limping, etc.) and one can reinforce healthy coping behaviour, by praising behaviour which is inconsistent with the sick role. One can encourage the patient's relatives to implement a similar kind of approach with the patient either on the ward or even at home. One can draw up a graph measuring the amount of 'up-time' that a patient spends in activity and encourage this to increase with time, again using praise as a reinforcer. The praise also increases the patient's level of self-esteem.

Teaching deep relaxation

Make sure that the patient is sitting or lying comfortably with his eyes closed, arms by his sides and legs uncrossed. Point out to him that it is important to focus on the word *relax*, relaxing each muscle group — trying to let the relaxation happen without forcing it. Breathing should be regular, shallow and relaxed. Draw attention to the fact that relaxation increases each time you breathe out. Breathe out through the nose steadily and regularly, concentrating on the word *relax* with every out-breath.

Then one can commence a series of exercises for each muscle group. In turn by tensing a set of muscles and then relaxing them the patient can be taught the difference between tension and relaxation.

Here is a set of exercises which can be worked through with the patient:

'First let us concentrate on the muscles in your arms and hands. You can tense these muscles by clenching your fists as tightly as possible and feeling tension in your hands and forearms. Tense your fists now — tight — tight — feel the tension in your hands and arms — feel the tension — and relax. Relax your hands and notice the difference between tension and relaxation in your hands and arms.

Let's try that exercise again. Let's try tensing the muscles in your hands and arms. You can tense these by clenching your fists as tightly as possible, and feel the difference between tension and relaxation. Tense your fists now, tight — tight — feel the tension in your hands and arms — feel the tension — and relax, and focus on the word relax while you let the muscles in your hands and arms relax more and more deeply. Concentrate on the feeling of letting go.

And now the muscles at the top of your arms. Tense these by bending your arms at the elbows, and try to touch your wrists to your shoulders. That's right — try and touch your wrists to your shoulders. Tense your muscles now, bend your wrists to your shoulders and tense the muscles in your arms as tightly as possible — tight — tight — feel the tension, hold it, and relax. Let your arms fall back by your side and notice the difference between tension and relaxation in your arms.

Let's do that exercise again and tense your muscles at the top of your arms by bending your arms at the elbows trying to touch your wrists to your shoulders. That's right, tense your muscles now, bring your wrists to your shoulders and tense the muscles in your arms as tightly as possible — tight — tight — feel the tension, hold it, and relax and let your muscles loosen and unwind more and more deeply. Carry on that feeling of letting go, letting the muscles become more and more relaxed and continue that feeling of relaxation throughout your arms. Let your arms loosen, unwind and relax.

And now the muscles in your shoulders. You can tense these by shrugging your shoulders, by drawing them up into your neck as tightly as you can. Try it now — that's right — hold it tight, tight, feel the tension in your shoulders, and relax. Let your shoulders drop and relax. Feel the tension ease away. Let your shoulders drop and relax and unwind and feel yourself relaxing more and more. We'll do that exercise again and tense the muscles in your shoulders by drawing them up into your neck as tightly as you can. Try it now — hold it tight — feel the tension in your shoulders — hold it — and relax. Let your shoulders drop and relax. Feel the tension ease away, feel yourself relaxing more and more, more and more. No effort, no tension. And continue with the feeling of letting go.

And now the muscles in your forehead and face. You can tense these muscles by screwing your face up as tightly as possible. Try it now — good — screw your face up as tightly as possible now, tight — tight — hold it, and relax. No tension in your face and forehead. Notice the difference between tension and relaxation and carry on the feeling of letting go, growing more and more deeply relaxed. And let's repeat that exercise again, and tense the muscles in your face by screwing up your face as tightly as possible, tense it now, good, tight — tight —hold it, and relax. No tension in your face and forehead. Notice the difference between tension and relaxation, and carry on that feeling of letting go—more and more relaxed. And carry on concentrating on the word relax, as you unwind more and more.

And now the muscles in your chest. You can tense these by taking in a deep breath, now breathe in as deeply as you can - hold it, feel the tension, feel the tension in your chest, and relax. Breathe right out and feel the relief of letting go. Breathing shallowly, not too deeply, and every time you breathe out, relax a little more. Let's do that exercise again by tensing the muscles in your chest. You can tense these by taking in a deep breath, now breathing in as deeply as you can, hold it — hold it — feel the tension in your chest and relax. Breathe right out and feel the relief of letting go. Breathing shallowly, not too deeply, and every time you breathe out, relax a little more. Let yourself unwind and let all the tension easy away.

And now the muscles at the top of your legs. You can tense these muscles by pressing your legs together as hard as possible. Try it now, tense your muscles, hold it — hold it — feel the tension and relax. Notice the difference between tension and relaxation as you carry on that feeling of letting go, more and more relaxed. Let's do that exercise again, and tense the muscles at the top of your legs by pressing your legs together as tightly as possible. Try it now, tense your muscles, hold it — hold it — feel the tension and relax. Notice the difference again between tension and relaxation as you carry on the feeling of letting go — more and more relaxed. And notice your breathing, each time you breathe out, relax a little more.

And now the muscles in your legs and feet. You can tense these muscles by straightening your legs and pointing your feet downwards, now, straighten your legs and point your feet down. Feel the tension, hold it — hold it — and relax. Relax your legs and let them loosen and unwind. Let's do that exercise again and tense the muscles in your legs and feet, by straightening your legs and pointing your feet downwards, now straighten your legs and point your feet down. Feel the tension hold it — hold it — and relax. Relax your legs and let them loosen and unwind. Concentrate on the feeling of relaxation, and notice the difference between tension and relaxation in your legs. Let the muscles in your legs feel more and more relaxed.

Now try and let that feeling of relaxation spread throughout all your body. Keep your breathing regular, shallow and relaxed. And every time you breathe out, relax a little more. Let the relaxation flow over you. Feel as if you were sinking, more and more deeply relaxed, comfortable, calm, and relaxed. No tension just relaxed, and let yourself go. And enjoy that feeling of relaxation for the next few moments as you unwind more and more. (120 second pause).

And now I am going to count backwards from 4 to 1. When I reach 1, open your eyes, sit up slowly, alert, refreshed and still feeling comfortably relaxed, 4. . . . . .3. . . . .2. . . . .1'

Adapted by kind permission of Research Press Inc. and the authors, from Bernstein, D.A. and Borkovec, T.D. (1973), pp. 21–23.

Distraction or attention diversion techniques

In the absence of muscular relaxation, one can teach distraction or attention diversion techniques.

1. Imaginative inattention, that is getting the patients to ignore the pain and imagine that they are on a beach instead.
2. Imaginative transformation of the pain allows the patient to acknowledge the noxious sensations but to interpret them as something other than pain or minimise them as trivial or unreal.

3. Imaginative transformation of context is when the patient imagines that he is in a 'James Bond' type scene and that the pain he is feeling is part of the action or drama.
4. Attention diversion (external)   Get the patient to focus on something in the environment, for example counting the ceiling tiles in the room.
5. Attention diversion (internal)   Get the patient to do mental arithmetic or make a list of popular songs.
6. Somatisation   Get the patient to focus on the part of the body receiving the intense stimulation and to analyse it as if he was going to write a biology report on it and thereby distance himself from it.

Although some of these techniques may be new to the patient, very probably offering a choice will help because in the past the patient may have (without even realising it) used similar kinds of coping skills already and will know which ones suit him best. You maximise the efficiency of treatment if you allow the patient to cooperate with you in a treatment alliance. One should discourage dependency and passivity and encourage the patient to take an active and independent part in the management of his pain.

CONCLUSION

Pain is a burden for the patient, but pain patients are tiring, arouse anxiety and guilt and drain the resources of all the staff trying to manage and treat their pain. This must be especially true for nurses who have greater and longer contact with patients than other health professionals.

A patient in pain can easily become irritated and distressed by the way other people react to his illness and envy their better health. Since he feels out of control of his own life he can feel hostility and suspicion towards others, blaming them for his difficulties and making attempts to manipulate and control others.

Alternatively, a patient may feel responsible for or that he deserves his pain. He may have difficulty in expressing personal feelings towards others, especially if those feelings are negative.

Nurses can do a great deal not only to alleviate the pain but also to help the person to cope with the pain. An understanding of the psychology of pain and knowing how damaging pain can be to the patient's body image, self-image and self-esteem can help the nurse to assess the patient accurately and facilitate the establishment of a treatment alliance, which will give the patient a feeling of being more in control. It should be remembered that many of the skills needed are already being utilised daily by nurses. It has been the aim of this chapter to make nurses more confident that they are understanding correctly the communications made to them by their patients and using the skills already within their repertoire to help ease the burden of pain for their patients.

REFERENCES

Bernstein, D.A. and Borkovec, T.D. (1973) *Progressive Relaxation Training.* Research Press, Champaign, Illinois.

Bond, M.R. (1979) *Pain, its Nature, Analysis and Treatment.* Churchill Livingstone, Edinburgh.

Crown, S. and Crisp, A.H. (1966) A short clinical diagnostic self-rating scale for psychoneurotic patients. The Middlesex Hospital Questionnaire (MHQ). *British Journal of Psychiatry,* **112**, 917–923.

Eysenck, H.J. and Eysenck, S.B.G. (1975) *Manual of the Eysenck Personality Questionnaire.* Hodder and Stoughton, London.

Melzack, R. (1975) The McGill Pain Questionnaire: major properties and scoring methods. *Pain,* **1**, 277–299.

Melzack, R. and Wall, P. (1988) *The Challenge of Pain,* 2nd edn. Penguin, London.

Pilowsky, I. and Spence, N.D. (1975) Patterns of illness behaviour in patients with intractable pain. (Includes the Illness Behaviour Questionnaire.) *Journal of Psychosomatic Research,* **19**, 279–287.

Snaith, R.P., Constantopoulos, A.A., Jardine, M.Y. and McGuffin, P. (1978) A Clinical scale for the self-assessment of irritability. *British Journal of Psychiatry,* **132**, 164–171.

Spielberger, C.D., Johnson, H.E. and Jacobs, G.A. (1982) Self-Analysis Questionnaire (AX). Unpublished, obtainable from Prof. C.D. Spielberger, Director, Centre for Research in Behavioural Medicine and Health Psychology, University of South Florida, Tampa 33623–8100, USA.

Tan, S. (1982) Cognitive and cognitive-behavioural methods for pain control: a selective review. *Pain,* **12**, 201–228.

Zigmond, A.S. and Snaith, R.P. (1983) The hospital anxiety and depression scale. *Acta Psychiatrica Scandinavica,* **67**, 361–370.

BIBLIOGRAPHY

Broome, A. and Jellicoe, H. (1987) *Living with Your Pain: A Guide to Managing Pain.* BPS/Methuen, Leicester.

Humphey, M. (1989) *Back Pain.* Routledge, London.

Tanschke, E., Merskey, H. and Helmes, E. (1990) Psychological defence mechanisms in patients with pain. *Pain,* **40**, 161–170.

Use of drugs 6
in pain control

The correct use of drugs in the management of pain is essential if effective pain control is to be achieved. However, all too frequently pain is poorly controlled because inappropriate and/or inadequate drug regimes have been implemented. The most common reasons for this problem occurring are:

- Inaccurate assessment of the presenting pain problem.
- A lack of insight into which drugs to use in the treatment of different types of pain as a result of inadequate knowledge about how analgesic drugs work.

The World Health Organisation (WHO) made a significant contribution in attempting to structure a practical and effective approach to cancer pain by devising an analgesic ladder (Rexed et al., 1984; WHO, 1986; Takeda, 1986). The principles recommended by the WHO can be utilised and adapted to clinical situations other than cancer where pain is a problem. Fig. 6.1 illustrates an example of an analgesic ladder used in clinical practice when treating many different pain syndromes.

Nurses not only have a responsibility for handling and administering drugs correctly when giving them to patients, but they also have a responsibility towards educating patients and their carers in the management of their own drugs. This chapter therefore discusses the drugs used in the management of different types of pain and also offers some useful reminders on the handling and administration of those drugs.

NON-STEROIDAL ANTI-INFLAMMATORY DRUGS (NSAIDs)

NSAIDS are recognised as an anti-inflammatory agent for both generalised and localised conditions and also as an

55

Fig. 6.1 An example of an analgesic ladder used in clinical practice.

IF PAIN PERSISTS REASSESS TYPE AND SEVERITY OF PAIN

IF PAIN PERSISTS REASSESS TYPE AND SEVERITY OF PAIN

NON-NARCOTIC
e.g., NSAID, paracetamol, aspirin

± ADJUVANT THERAPY
e.g.,
(i) Corticosteroids
(ii) Central drugs
e.g., tricyclic anti-convulsants
(iii) Psychotropic drugs
e.g., phenothiazines
(iv) Simple local anaesthetic techniques, e.g., trigger point injections, intra-articular injections

---

IF OPIATE RESPONSIVE
GIVE WEAK NARCOTIC
e.g., co-proxamol, codeine, dihydrocodeine

± NSAID

IF NOT OPIATE RESPONSIVE
± ADJUVANT THERAPY
e.g., as before (i)–(iv), plus,
(v) Neural blockade, e.g., local anaesthetic, neurolytic

IF OPIATE RESPONSIVE
GIVE STRONG NARCOTIC
e.g., temgesic, phenazocine, morphine, diamorphine

± co-proxamol
dihydrocodeine } for break-through pain
dextromoramide

± NSAID

IF NOT OPIATE RESPONSIVE
± ADJUVANT THERAPY
e.g., as before (i)–(v)

IF PAIN RESOLVES REASSESS ANALGESIC THERAPY

IF PAIN RESOLVES REASSESS ANALGESIC THERAPY

ACTIVE CLINICAL THERAPY ⟹ PALLIATIVE CONTINUING CARE

analgesic (Zoppi and Zamponi, 1988). They are particularly useful in the treatment of bone pain caused by conditions such as arthritis or bone metastases. This is because pain associated with these conditions is thought to be due to the excessive liberation of prostaglandins and NSAIDs directly inhibit the release of prostaglandins.

Side effects

Irritation of gastric mucosa
Nausea and vomiting
Diarrhoea
Iron deficiency anaemia in long-term use because of very small blood loss that occurs in approximately 70% of patients
Hypersensitivity reactions, for example angioedema, bronchospasm and rashes
Headache
Vertigo
Tinnitus

Contra-indications

Anti-coagulant therapy
Haemophilia
Previous history of gastric mucosal lesion, for example an ulcer
Impaired renal or liver function

To reduce the risk of gastric irritation some of the precautions available are:

1. Always take NSAIDs with milk or after meals.
2. Concurrent therapy of a synthetic analogue of prostaglandin E1 (alprostadil), such as cytotec, to inhibit gastric acid secretion.
3. Concurrent therapy of an H_2 receptor blocker, such as ranitidine or cimetidine, to reduce gastric acid secretion.

When using NSAIDs the benefits always have to be balanced with the possibility of incidence of side effects. Inherently, the stronger the NSAID the greater possibility there is of side effects.

Differences in anti-flammatory activity between NSAIDs are small, but there is considerable variation in individual patient response. It can therefore mean trying different NSAIDs to find one that suits each patient being treated. A positive response should occur within a few days of commencing treatment. If no improvement is seen after one week when requiring analgesic response, or after three weeks when requiring anti-inflammatory response, then the NSAID should be changed.

Aspirin

Preparations available
Tablet, soluble tablet, slow-release tablet and enteric-coated tablet. In some hospitals it is possible to obtain a suppository preparation.

Dose
Visceral pain: 600 mg, 4–6 hourly.
Rheumatoid arthritis: 900 mg–1.2g, 4–6 hourly.

Additional contra-indication
Aspirin is no longer recommended in children under 12 years and in breast-feeding unless specifically indicated, for example juvenile rheumatoid arthritis. This is because of evidence of possible links in these groups between aspirin administration and Reyes syndrome.

Benorylate (Benoral)

Benorylate is an ester of aspirin and paracetamol, which has some anti-inflammatory properties in addition to analgesic properties.

Dose
1.5–2 g, 8 hourly.

Side effects
These resemble those associated with aspirin rather than paracetamol. The risk of hepatotoxity may be less than with paracetamol.

Indomethacin (Indocid)

Preparations available
Capsule, slow-release tablet, suspension and suppository. Intravenous preparation is available only for neonates in the treatment of patent ductus arteriosus.

Dose
Oral: 50–200 mg daily in divided doses.
Rectal: 100 mg at night and in the morning if required.

In combined oral and rectal treatment the maximum total daily dose is 150–200 mg.

Diclofenac sodium (Voltarol)

Preparations available
Tablet, slow-release tablet, injection and suppository.

Dose
Oral: 75–150 mg daily in 2–3 divided doses.
Rectal: 100 mg usually at night.
Intramuscular injection: 75 mg daily which can be increased to twice daily in severe cases for a maximum of 2 days.

The maximum total daily dose by any route is 150 mg.

Ketoprofen (Orudis, Oruvail)

Preparations available
Capsule, slow-release capsule and suppository.

Dose
Oral: 100–200 mg daily in 2–4 divided doses.
Rectal: 100 mg at night.

In combined oral and rectal treatment the maximum total daily dose is 200 mg.

Piroxicam (Feldene)

Preparations available
Capsule, dispersible tablet, suppository and gel.

Dose
20 mg initially. 10–30 mg daily maintenance dose in single or divided doses. In acute conditions 40 mg daily can be given for 2 days, then 20 mg maintenance dose.
Gel: 1 g (3 cm) 3–4 times daily, to be reviewed after 4 weeks.

Naproxyn (Naprosyn)

Preparations available
Tablet, suspension, granules and suppository.

Dose
Oral: 500 mg–1 g daily in 2 divided doses.
Rectal: 500 mg at night and in the morning if required.

The maximum total daily dose is 1 g.

Ibuprofen (Brufen)

Preparations available
Tablet, slow-release capsule and syrup.

Dose
Initially 1.2–1.8 g daily in 3–4 divided doses.
This can be increased if necessary to 2.4 g daily. A maintenance dose of 0.6–1.2 g daily may be adequate.

Flurbiprofen (Froben)

Preparations available
Tablet, slow-release capsule and suppository.

Dose
150–200 mg daily in divided doses.
In acute conditions this can be increased to 300 mg daily.

Sulindac (Clinoril)

Preparation available
Tablet.

Dose
200 mg twice daily, which may be reduced according to response.

Fenbufen (Lederfen, Traxam)

Preparations available
Tablet, effervescent tablet, capsule and gel.

Dose
300 mg in the morning and 600 mg at night or 450 mg twice daily.
Gel: 2–4 times daily for up to 14 days. Maximum daily application 25 g.

Diflunisal (Dolobid)

Preparation available
Tablet.

Dose
Initially 1 g daily in 2 divided doses, then 0.5–1 g daily.
The maximum total daily dose is 1.5 g.

Mefenamic acid (Ponstan)

Preparations available
Tablet, tablet forte, dispersible tablet and capsule.

Dose
500 mg 3 times daily.

Phenylbutazone (Butacote, Butazolidin)

Preparations available
Tablet, enteric-coated tablet.

Dose
Initially 200 mg 2–3 times daily, then reduce to effective minimum dose, usually 100 mg 2–3 times daily.

SIMPLE ANALGESICS

Drugs in this group act mainly peripherally and are useful for mild to moderate visceral pain.

Aspirin

Aspirin is both an analgesic agent and an anti-inflammatory agent (see NSAIDs).

Paracetamol

Paracetamol is equipotent to aspirin for its analgesic properties, but it has no anti-inflammatory properties.

Preparations available
Tablet, soluble tablet and suspension. In some hospitals it is possible to obtain a suppository preparation.

Dose
0.5–1 g 4–6 hourly. The maximum daily dose is 4 g.

Side effects
Hepatotoxicity on prolonged use or overdosage. Side effects otherwise are usually mild and only rarely haematological reactions, skin rashes and other allergic reactions occur. Paracetamol is less gastric-irritant than aspirin.

Contra-indications
Impaired liver function.

Benorylate (Benoral)

Benorylate is both an analgesic agent and an anti-inflammatory agent (see NSAIDs).

NARCOTIC ANALGESICS

The use of narcotic analgesics should be instigated when visceral or potentially opiate responsive pain has proved resistant to non-narcotic therapy. It should, however, be stressed that narcotic analgesics should not be commenced when a patient has an opiate non-responsive pain, for example neurogenic or bone pain. Narcotic analgesics act mainly centrally on the perception of pain by the brain, whereas simple analgesics act mainly peripherally. It is important to remember that there are two major groups of narcotic analgesics available:

1. Narcotic agonists. Drugs in this group stimulate the opiate receptors. Side effects such as respiratory depression can be reversed using naloxone.
2. Narcotic agonist–antagonists. Drugs in this group stimulate the opiate receptors (agonist) when used alone but are thought to act as receptor blockers (antagonist) when combined with other narcotic agonist analgesics. Side effects such as respiratory depression are only partially reversed by naloxone, but doxapram may be used to reverse profound respiratory depression.

It is thought at the present time to be inadvisable to mix these two groups of narcotic analgesics if optimum pain control is to be achieved, but current research may change this thinking in the future.

Side effects

Constipation
Nausea and vomiting
Sedation
Dizziness
Respiratory depression
Suppression of cough reflex

Urinary retention
Enhancement of alcohol tolerance
Dependence

All these side effects can occur in varying degrees with different preparations, different routes and individual patient response. Many of these problems, however, can be overcome by using the most effective, appropriate route of administration and also by using the appropriate co-adjuvant drugs, for example laxative and anti-emetic drugs.

In the first few days of chronic administration some side effects, for example nausea and sedation, can resolve spontaneously. It is therefore important to reassess this situation continuously as co-adjuvants such as anti-emetics may not necessarily be required as long-term therapy.

Caution should be taken in the following situations:

Raised intra-cranial pressure or head injury
Hypotension
Hypothyroidism
Asthma
Decreased respiratory reserve
Hepatic and renal impairment
Pregnancy
Breast-feeding
Drug abuse history

When managing opiate-sensitive pain in the terminally ill these cautions should not necessarily be a deterrent to the use of narcotic analgesics. A sensible approach, balancing the benefits with the possibility of side effects, should be adopted.

NARCOTIC AGONISTS FOR MODERATE TO SEVERE VISCERAL PAIN

Codeine phosphate

Codeine phosphate is less likely to depress the respiratory centre, and is a useful drug for patients who have head injuries.

Preparations available
Tablet and syrup which are not controlled drugs.
Injection which is a controlled drug.

Dose
30–60 mg 4–6 hourly. The maximum total daily dose is 180 mg.

Dihydrocodeine (DF118)

Dihydrocodeine is slightly more potent than codeine orally, but it causes more constipation.

Preparations available
Tablet, slow-release tablet and elixir which are not controlled drugs.
Injection which is a controlled drug.

Dose
Oral: 30–60 mg 4–6 hourly.
Injection: up to 50 mg 4–6 hourly.

Dextropropoxyphene

Given alone, dextropropoxyphene is less potent than codeine, but in combination with other preparations, for example paracetamol and aspirin, it has a more powerful effect (see Compound analgesic preparations).

Preparation available
Capsule.

Dose
65 mg 6–8 hourly.

Compound analgesic preparations

Combination analgesics can be beneficial for some patients, however, they are not so flexible when considering raising the dose or adding co-adjuvant therapy. It should be remembered that the side effects of each individual component of the compound can still occur.

Dose
1–2 tablets 4–6 hourly. The maximum total daily dose is 8 tablets.

Examples of compound preparations available on prescription are:

Co-codamol
Preparations available:
   Tablet, dispersible tablet.
Compounds:
   Codeine phosphate 8 mg
   Paracetamol 500 mg

Co-codaprin
Preparations available:
   Tablet, dispersible tablet.
Compounds:
   Codeine phosphate 8 mg
   Aspirin 400 mg

Co-dydramol
Preparation available:
   Tablet.
Compounds:
   Dihydrocodeine tartrate 10 mg
   Paracetamol 500 mg

Co-proxamol
Preparation available:
   Tablet.
Compounds:
   Dextropropoxyphene 32.5 mg
   Paracetamol 325 mg

Many other proprietary analgesic preparations are available, but they are not available on NHS prescriptions.

NARCOTIC AGONISTS FOR
SEVERE VISCERAL PAIN

All preparations within this group are controlled drugs.

Morphine

Morphine is the standard of narcotic against which others are compared. The recommended dose is to use whatever controls the pain, titrating the initial dose to the patient's previous use of opiates, the individual clinical situation and thus the potential side effects. No upper limit per dose is recognised in palliative care. However, if dosage increases rapidly without adequate pain relief a check-list should always be worked through before increasing the opiate dose any further. For example:

1. Is it the type of pain that responds to opiates?
2. Are the appropriate co-adjuvant therapies being used?
3. Is the drug being administered via the most effective and appropriate route?
4. Are there any other contributing factors clinically, for example abnormal urea and electrolytes?
5. What is the psychological state of the patient?

Potency ratios of different routes
It is important to be aware that different routes of administration have different potency ratios.

1. Intramuscular (IM) Subcutaneous (SC) routes
   Acute
   IM/SC morphine given as a single injection in an acute situation is thought to be six times more potent than the oral route, for example:
   10 mg IM/SC morphine = 60 mg oral morphine.
   Chronic
   IM/SC morphine in chronic administration is thought to be two to three times more potent than the oral route, for example:
   10 mg IM/SC morphine = 20–30 mg oral morphine.
2. Intravenous (IV) route
   Acute
   IV morphine given as a single injection in an acute situation is ·

thought to be six to eight times more potent than the oral route, for example:

10 mg IV morphine = 60–80 mg oral morphine.

Chronic

Morphine is not usually given IV in chronic administration because of the rapid onset of tolerance.

3. Epidural route

   Epidural morphine is thought to be 10 times more potent than the oral route, for example:

   10 mg epidural morphine = 100 mg oral morphine.

4. Intrathecal morphine

   Intrathecal morphine is thought to be 100 times more potent than the oral route, for example:

   10 mg intrathecal morphine = 1000 mg (1 g) oral morphine.

Preparations available

MST Continus: Slow-release tablets available in 10, 30, 60 and 100 mg preparations. Starting dose: 10–30 mg 12 hourly.

Oramorph: Oral solution available in 10 mg/5 ml and 100 mg/5 ml. Starting dose: 5–10 mg 4 hourly.

Morphine elixir: Diluted in chloroform water base. Starting dose: 5–10 mg 4 hourly.

Morphine sulphate injection: Available in 10, 15 and 30 mg/ml. Starting dose: 2.5–10 mg 4 hourly.

Morphine suppositories: Available in 15 mg preparation. The dose is 15–30 mg 4 hourly.

A parenteral preparation of morphine is available without preservatives for epidural and intrathecal use. Preparations of morphine with other additives included, for example an anti-emetic, are not usually advisable because all the components have to be increased or decreased together when a change in morphine dose is required.

Diamorphine

Diamorphine is thought to be equipotent to morphine and is equal in terms of addictive properties. It causes relatively less nausea and hypotension. The biggest advantage of diamorphine over morphine is its greater solubility. Doses, oral/injectable potency ratios and problems of diamorphine preparations with additives are as with morphine.

Preparations available

Diamorphine tablets: Available in 10 mg preparation. Starting dose: 5–10 mg 4 hourly.

Diamorphine elixir: Diluted in chloroform water base. Starting dose: 5–10 mg 4 hourly.

Diamorphine injection: Available in 5, 10, 30, 100 and 500 mg ampoules of powder for reconstitution. Starting dose: 2.5–10 mg 4 hourly.

Diamorphine injection can also be used for epidural and intrathecal use.

Dextromoramide (Palfium)

Dextromoramide has a very quick onset of action but has a short duration of action. It is useful for breakthrough pain in addition to regular baseline analgesia.

5 mg dextromoramide = 10 mg morphine.

Preparations available

Tablet, injection and suppository.

Dose

Oral: 5–20 mg 2–3 hourly as required.

Injection: 5–15 mg IM/SC 2–3 hourly as required.

Rectal: 10 mg 2–3 hourly as required.

Pethidine

Pethidine has a quick onset of action with a short duration of action.

100 mg pethidine = 10 mg morphine

Preparations available

Tablet and injection. A parenteral preparation of pethidine is available without preservatives for epidural and intrathecal use.

Dose

Oral: 50–150 mg 4 hourly.

Injection: 25–100 mg IM/SC 4 hourly.
25–50 mg slow IV 4 hourly.

While pethidine is recommended 4 hourly the recognised therapeutic life is only 2–3 hours.

Omnopon (Papaveretum)

Omnopon is a mixed opium alkaloid which is particularly popular as a pre-medication pre-operatively and as a post-operative analgesic. It has some muscle relaxant properties.

20 mg omnopon = 13.4 mg morphine.

Preparation available
Injection.

Dose
10–20 mg IM/SC 4 hourly.
2.5–5 mg slow IV 4 hourly.

Phenazocine (Narphen)

Phenazocine is particularly useful for biliary colic and pancreatic pain because it has less tendency to increase biliary pressure than other narcotics.

5 mg phenazocine = 15–25 mg morphine, depending on the preparation of morphine given.

Preparation available
Tablet.

Dose
Oral or sublingual: 5 mg 4–6 hourly.
Single doses may be increased to 20 mg.
Sublingual administration can reduce the incidence of nausea and vomiting.

Methadone (Physeptone)

Methadone is a long-acting narcotic which is less sedating than morphine. The major problem is that it can accumulate when administered over a long period of time. The linctus preparation is particularly useful when treating cough in terminal disease.

Methadone mixture is two and a half times the strength of methadone linctus with other additives. It should only be used as an alternative to other narcotics such as diamorphine as part of a planned programme of opiate withdrawal for drug dependents.

Preparations available
Tablet, linctus, mixture and injection.

Dose
Oral: Tablet, 5–10 mg 6–8 hourly.
Linctus: 1–2 mg (2.5–5 ml) 4–6 hourly.
Injection: 5–10 mg IM/SC 6–8 hourly.

In long-term administration the dose should be reduced to twice daily because of the accummulatory effects.

Oxycodone pectinate (Proladone)

Oxycodone is a useful long-acting narcotic.
30 mg oxycodone pectinate = 10 mg morphine.

Preparation available
Suppository.

Dose
Rectal: 30 mg 8–12 hourly.

Fentanyl (Sublimaze)

Fentanyl is a useful analgesic drug both peri-operatively and for the ventilated/critically ill patient undergoing continual monitoring. It may produce severe respiratory depression, particularly when patients have decreased respiratory function or when other respiratory depressant drugs have been given. Fentanyl is thought to be approximately 100 times more potent than morphine.

Preparation available
Injection.

Dose
50–200 μg IV then 50 μg as required.
300–500 μg IV for the ventilated patient.
Continuous IV or epidural infusion can also be administered effectively.

Alfentanil (Rapifen)

Alfentanil is a shorter acting drug than fentanyl.

Preparation available
Injection.

Dose
500 μg IV initially, then up to 250 μg every 4–5 minutes as required.
Infusion for ventilated patients: 50–100 μg per kg over 10 minutes.

NARCOTIC AGONIST-ANTAGONISTS FOR MODERATE TO SEVERE PAIN

Pentazocine (Fortral)

Pentazocine is more potent than codeine or dihydrocodeine in injection form, but side effects such as hallucinations and thought disturbances have meant that it is now not recommended as an analgesic drug of choice.

Preparations available
Tablet, capsule, injection and suppository.

Dose
Oral: 50 mg 3–4 hourly (range 25–100 mg).
Injection: 30–60 mg SC/IM/IV 3–4 hourly.
Rectal: 50 mg up to 4 times daily.

Buprenorphine (Temgesic)

Buprenorphine is a longer-acting drug with potentially lower dependence compared to morphine. The main side effect is nausea and vomiting. Buprenorphine is now a schedule 3 controlled drug (see Useful Reminders, 18).

0.4 mg buprenorphine = 16–20 mg morphine.

Preparations available
Sublingual tablet and injection.

Dose
Sublingual: 200–400 μg 6–8 hourly.
Injection: 300–600 μg 6–8 hourly.

CORTICOSTEROIDS

Corticosteroids are useful anti-inflammatory/analgesic drugs in clinical situations such as:
1. Oedema and inflammation from malignant tumour which cause, for example:
    Nerve compression
    Lymphoedema
    Gastro-intestinal obstruction
    Headache from raised intra-cranial pressure
2. Benign inflammatory processes, for example:
    Generalised and localised inflammatory conditions of the joints such as rheumatoid disease.
    Localised soft tissue inflammatory conditions such as golfer's or tennis elbow and tendinitis.

Side effects

The following side effects can occur in varying degrees depending on the preparation used, the time scale of therapy and individual response:

Fluid retention
Hypertension
Gastric irritation
Paranoia
Muscle weakness

Cushing's syndrome
Diabetes
Osteoporosis

As with NSAIDs and narcotics a sensible approach to corticosteroid therapy has to be adopted, balancing benefits with potential side effects. Precautions and/or co-adjuvant therapies should be initiated as appropriate.

Dexamethasone (Oradexon, Decadron)

Dexamethasone is useful when there is acute exacerbation of clinical situations outlined in 1. above due to malignant disease process. It is particularly useful because it crosses the blood–brain barrier. Dexamethasone can also be helpful in the treatment of local inflammation of joints and soft tissue.

Preparations available
Tablet and injection.

Dose
1. Malignant disease: It is advisable to start on a high dose, for example 16 mg daily in divided doses, and reduce over several days to a maintenance dose such as 2–4 mg daily. With some patients the drug can be discontinued after an acute clinical episode.
2. Benign local inflammatory disease: 0.4 mg by intra-articular, intralesional or soft tissue injection at intervals of 3–21 days according to response.

Prednisolone (various tablet trade names, Deltastab=injection)

Prednisolone is useful for generalised inflammation and local inflammation of joints and soft tissue. It is sometimes given in conjunction with or instead of NSAIDs.

Preparations available
Tablet, enteric-coated tablet, soluble tablet and injection.

Dose
Oral: Up to 30 mg daily in divided doses.
Injection: 25–100 mg IM once or twice weekly.
5–25 mg by intra-articular, intrasynovial or soft tissue injection. Not more than three joints should be treated on the same day.

Hydrocortisone acetate (Hydrocortistab)

Hydrocortisone acetate is used for local inflammation of joints and soft tissue.

Preparation available
Injection.

Dose
5–50 mg by intra-articular, intrasynovial or soft tissue injection. Not more than three joints should be treated on the same day.

Methylprednisolone acetate (Depo-Medrone)

Methylprednisolone acetate is a useful anti-inflammatory preparation which lasts for longer periods of time.

Preparation available
Injection.

Dose
40–80 mg by intra-articular, intrasynovial or soft tissue injection, which can be repeated every 1–5 weeks according to response. In malignant disease in some situations the dose can be increased to 120 mg.

CENTRAL-ACTING DRUGS

Central-acting drugs are essential in the treatment of neurogenic pain, for example:

1.   Malignant disease with neurogenic involvement

2. Post-herpetic neuralgia
3. Trigeminal neuralgia
4. Thalamic syndrome

They are also useful in improving mood and sleep at night which can help the patient cope with the pain more positively. This may be particularly helpful if there is a depressive component to the pain syndrome. It is important to educate the patient into under-standing that the benefits of this group of drugs on the pain will not be felt immediately and that it is important to persist with the treatment.

Side effects

It is important to explain to the patient that side effects may occur initially, but will gradually decrease over a week or two. For this reason also it is important to stress the need to persist with the treatment. Possible side effects are:

Sedation
Drowsiness
Dry mouth
Arrhythmias and heart block
Constipation
Urinary retention
Sweating
Convulsions
Hepatic reactions
Haematological reactions
Blurred vision

Contra-indications

Recent myocardial infarction
Heart block
Mania
Porphyria

Caution should be taken in the following situations:

Antidepressants may interfere with antihypertensive therapy
Effects of alchohol may be increased
Sedation may affect the ability to drive or operate machinery
Diabetes
Epilepsy
Pregnancy and breast feeding
Hepatic impairment
Thyroid disease
Psychoses
Glaucoma
Urinary retention

Dose

Doses are usually judged on individual patient response, commencing on a lower dose and gradually increasing over a period of time.

Tricylic anti-depressants

Amitriptyline hydrochloride (Domical, Lentizol, Tryptizol)
Preparations available:
   Tablet, slow-release capsule, mixture and injection.
Dose:
   Oral: Initially 25–75 mg at night or divided daily doses.
   It can be increased gradually to 150–250 mg daily.
   Usual maintenance dose is 50–100 mg daily.
   Injection: 10–20 mg IM/IV 4 times daily.

Dothiepin hydrochloride (Prothiadin)
Preparations available:
   Tablet and capsule.
Dose:
   Initially 25–75 mg at night or divided daily doses.
   It can be increased gradually to 150 mg daily, and up to 225 mg daily in hospital patients.

Imipramine hydrochloride (Tofranil)
Preparations available:
   Tablet and syrup.

Dose:

Initially 25–75 mg in divided doses.

It can be increased gradually to 200 mg daily and up to 225 mg in hospital patients.

Up to 150 mg may be given as a single dose at night.

Nortriptyline (Allegron, Aventyl)
Preparations available:

Tablet, capsule and liquid.

Dose:

20–40 mg daily in divided doses.

It can be increased gradually to 100 mg daily.

Usual maintenance dose is 30–75 mg daily.

Mianserin hydrochloride (Bolvidon, Norval)
Preparation available:

Tablet.

Dose:

Initially 30–40 mg at night or divided daily doses.

It can be increased gradually up to 90 mg daily.

Particular caution:

Mianserin has particularly been associated with leucopenia, agranulocytosis and aplastic anaemia. Monthly full blood counts are therefore recommended during the first three months of treatment with subsequent monitoring as appropriate.

Trazodone hydrochloride (Molipaxin)
Preparations available:

Tablet, capsule and liquid.

Dose:

100–150 mg at night or divided daily doses.

It can be increased to 200–300 mg daily and up to 600 mg daily in hospital patients.

Compound anti-depressants

This group of drugs is a combination of anti-depressant and phenothiazine. It is therefore important to remember that when increasing and decreasing the dose both components will be affected.

Motival
fluphenazine hydrochloride	500 μg
nortriptyline	10 mg

Motipress
fluphenazine hydrochloride	1.5 mg
nortriptyline	30 mg

Triptafen
perphenazine	2 mg
amitriptyline hydrochloride	25 mg

Anti-epileptics

This group of drugs is particularly useful in the treatment of trigeminal neuralgia.

Carbamazepine (Tegretol)
Preparations available:
    Tablet, slow-release tablet and liquid.
Dose:
    100 mg initially once or twice daily.
    It can be increased gradually to 200 mg 3–4 times daily.
    A total daily dosage of up to 1.6 g may be required.

Sodium valproate (Epilim)
Preparations available:
    Tablet, liquid, syrup and injection.
Dose:
    Initially 600 mg daily in divided doses, preferably after food.
    It can be increased gradually by 200 mg per day at 3 day intervals to a maximum of 2.5 g daily in divided doses.

Phenytoin (Epanutin)
Preparations available:
    Tablet, capsule, chewable tablet and suspension.
Dose:
    150–300 mg daily as a single dose or in divided doses.

It can be increased gradually as necessary, the usual dose is 300–400 mg daily.

The maximum dose is 600 mg daily.

USEFUL REMINDERS

1. Analgesic is the term used to describe a drug that relieves pain.
2. It is advisable to ensure drug therapy regimes are kept to a minimum number of drugs and that dosage schedules are as simple as possible. Drugs that interact, or combinations that could enhance side effects, should not be prescribed. Avoidance of multiple therapy minimuses the risk of such potential problems.
3. Pharmacists are a source of information should there be a query concerning drug therapy. The Drug Information Department in hospitals is a specific, easily accessible resource point for both hospital and community based nurses.
4. Drugs have Approved and Trade names. It is preferable to use Approved names.
5. Prescribing using instructions in latin should be discouraged as they can be misinterpreted. For example, 'b.d.', twice a day, 'nocté', at night.
6. Never exceed the dose stated on the label and read the directions carefully.
7. Further instructions on the label, for example advice on alcohol intake, should be noted.
8. Safe storage of all medicines must be observed in the home environment, for example:
   Keep out of the reach of children
   Do not store drugs in the bathroom or another warm, moist area as they absorb water.
   Hoarding of different drugs is not recommended.
   Always check a drug's expiry date.
   Never share drugs between household members.
9. Drugs should never be exchanged between patients.
10. Patients who suffer disabling diseases such as rheumatoid arthritis should request that their medicines be put in containers that they can open, and not ones with childproof caps.

11. The choice of formulation of a drug, for example oral, slow release or suppository, and the route of administration for example oral, intravenous, epidural or rectal should be carefully chosen as they may be essential in achieving maximum pain control and patient acceptability.

12. Some analgesics have side effects such as nausea, constipation or drowsiness which will either decrease as the therapy continues or can be controlled by appropriate co-adjuvant therapy.

13. Some analgesics can be purchased from a pharmacy without a prescription and may be suitable for first-line therapy.

14. It may be cheaper to purchase some analgesic prescriptions from a pharmacy than pay a prescription charge with an FP.10, for example simple analgesics and topical analgesic preparations.

15. Care should be taken when purchasing some medicines, for example cold remedies, to ensure that they do not contain the same drug as is already being taken and/or that they do not interact with or are contra-indicated with existing medication.

16. The concern about addiction to controlled analgesic drugs is a myth if the drugs are being used correctly for an indicated problem.

17. The 1971 Misuse of Drugs Act was passed to provide more flexible and comprehensive control over activities related to 'Controlled Drugs'. Three classes of drugs were identified.

18. The 1985 Misuse of Drugs Regulations define the classes of people authorised to supply and possess controlled drugs while acting in their professional capacities and lay down the conditions under which these activities may be carried out. Certain drugs may be more or less controlled depending on their formulation. It should be noted that the same drug may be a controlled drug in one form, but not in another. The law is subject to change with individual drugs. Of the 5 schedules identified in the Regulations, schedules 2 and 3 particularly apply to analgesics.

Schedule 2: drugs that are subject to the full controlled drug requirements relating to prescription writing, safe custody and the need to keep registers etc., for example, diamorphine, morphine, pethidine, injectable pentazocine.

Schedule 3: drugs that are subject to the special prescription requirements, but not the safe custody requirements or the need to keep registers. Invoices, however, require to be kept for two years, for example, buprenorphine and oral pentazocine.

19. Within hospitals the nurse in charge is responsible for the safe administration and storage of controlled drugs given to patients.

20. In the home environment controlled drugs are the property of the patient. Education is therefore essential in their use, safe storage and destruction.

REFERENCES

Rexed, B., Edmondson, K., Khan, I. and Sampson, R.J. (1984) Guidelines for the control of narcotic and psychotropic substances. In *The Context of International Treaties*, World Health Organization, Geneva.

Takeda, F. (1986) Results of field-testing in Japan of the WHO Draft Interim Guideline on relief of cancer pain. *The Pain Clinic*, 1, 83–89.

World Health Organization (1986) *Comprehensive Management of Cancer Pain*, World Health Organization, Geneva.

Zoppi, M. and Zamponi, A. (1988) Non-steroidal anti-inflammatory drugs. In 3rd International Symposium, 'The Pain Clinic', Florence, Italy, 11 September 1988.

BIBLIOGRAPHY

British Medical Association (1990) *British National Formulary*. British Medication Association and the Pharmaceutical Society of Great Britain.

Burton, S. and Jones, A. (1985) Pain Control — an Update on Drugs, King's College Hospital Information sheet.

Dale, J.R. and Applebe, G.E. (1987) *Pharmacy, Law and Ethics* (4th edn). The Pharmaceutical Press, UK.

Laurence, D.R. (1987) *Clinical Pharmacology* (6th edn). Churchill Livingstone, Edinburgh.

Twycross, R. and Lock, S. (1984) *Oral Morphine in Advanced Cancer*. Beaconsfield Publications.

Infusion pumps 7

The number of infusion pumps available for administering analgesic regimes is increasing all the time. Whilst this widens the choice for clinicians, it also poses the problem of deciding which is the most appropriate, efficient and reliable pump for different clinical situations.

A useful source of information on infusion equipment is the Department of Health Official Evaluation Centre, where all infusion pumps are tested. The 'Useful Addresses' section on p. 120 gives details of how to contact the Centre if information is required.

This chapter discusses routes of administration via infusion pumps, drug therapy, and different types of infusion pumps available for various clinical situations.

ROUTES OF ADMINISTRATION

Subcutaneous infusion

This is the route by which many patients, in particular the terminally ill, have their infusion administered. The cannula can be inserted into areas of the body such as the chest, upper arm or abdomen. Placement can often be influenced by the patient's disease process, for example:

1. Absorption of drugs may not occur effectively in an oedematous area.
2. A cannula cannot be placed into an area of broken skin.
3. Some localised areas may be more painful than others, for example, the chest wall with lung or breast cancer, and these areas should be avoided.

Patients often decide on the site of the cannula themselves after consultation so that it will interfere as little as possible with the life style they are able to enjoy.

Infusion sets
Examples of sets that may be used are:

1. 'Y' Cannula, 21 g/23 g.
2. Vygon 246.100 Butterfly Infusion Set, 21 g/23 g.

Both sets can have lengths of manometer tubing attached to them so that the system can be tailor made to the patient's needs.

The advantage of 'Y' cannulas is that the metal introducer is withdrawn and does not stay in the subcutaneous tissue, whereas with the butterfly cannulas the metal needle stays in the tissue. The possibility of localised tissue reaction is therefore thought to be minimised with a 'Y' cannula, and the optimum comfort is offered to the patient.

Introduction of the cannula
1. Prior to introduction of the cannula the area should be cleaned thoroughly with a medi-swab or equivalent cleaning solution.
2. The cannula should be inserted at 45° to the skin and laid flat.
3. Op-site, or an equivalent dressing, should be used to seal the area.

Care of the site
The area should be checked regularly, for example when the syringe is changed, to ensure that the tissue has not become inflamed or infected. Should this occur, or should the cannula block, a new cannula should be inserted at a different site.

The cannula can usually be left in place for one or two weeks, but because of the inevitably deteriorating condition of patients with terminal disease, it is important that regular assessment is made of each patient.

If is also important to remember that other factors may account for inflammation of the tissue, such as the drugs which are being administered.

The following cannot be used in a subcutaneous infusion pump because they are too irritant:
Prochlorperazine
Chlorpromazine
Diazepam
Dexamethasone

Intravenous infusion

Intravenous analgesic infusions can be useful in the management of post-operative and acute pain control. Whilst it can be useful in a selective number of patients who are terminally ill, it should be remembered that long-term intravenous therapy is inappropriate due to the problem of tolerance occurring.

Routine care of an intravenous site is required, and nurses changing the infusion must have gained their employing authority's certificate for intravenous drug administration because the procedure is within the extended role of the nurse.

Epidural infusion

Epidural analgesic infusions can be useful in acute pain, for example post-operative pain, and also in chronic pain, for example the terminally ill cancer or vascular patient. It should, however, be recognised that it is only a small number of palliative care patients who require analgesia by this route.

Care of the epidural catheter is discussed on p. 98, and nurses changing the infusion must have gained their employing authority's certificate for epidural drug administration because the procedure is within the extended role of the nurse.

DRUGS

Research has shown that care needs to be taken when mixing drugs due to varying degrees of incompatibility becoming evident (Regnard *et al*, 1986). A knowledge of drugs that can be used in the infusion pump and their idiosyncrasies is therefore essential if full potential of the regimes that can be used is to be realised. This has particular relevance with the advent of more slowly running long-term infusion pump regimes.

Care should be taken to store the syringe as much as possible away from light and the solution should be checked daily for precipitation or crystallisation.

Examples of drugs that can be used in terminal disease

Analgesics
Diamorphine and morphine sulphate can be used in whatever dose is needed for each individual patient. The advantage of diamorphine over morphine is its greater solubility. For potency ratios by different routes, see p. 67.

Anti-emetics
1. Droperidol   This is a useful anti-emetic that is used in preference to haloperidol.
2. Metoclopramide   This has been shown to have signs of degradation after one week of use. It is therefore not advisable to use it for periods longer than one week.
3. Cyclizine and haloperidol   Research has shown evidence of precipitation and crystallisation within a short period of time with both of these anti-emetics. It is therefore advisable only to infuse these drugs in low concentrates, for example, cyclizine 25 mg/ml, and haloperidol 2 mg/ml, over a period not exceeding 24 hours. Neither of these drugs is thought to be suitable for long-term pump regimes.
4. Hyoscine   This appears to remain stable over long periods of time in a syringe. It is therefore thought to be an ideal anti-emetic for long-term, slow-running regimes.
    The other properties for which it can be useful are as an anti-spasmodic and drying agent.
5. Methotrimeprazine   This is an extremely effective anti-emetic. Should higher concentrations than 100 mg be required it should be well diluted, to lessen the risk of skin irritation.

Local anaesthetics
Local anaesthetics, for example Marcain, can be administered by the epidural route.

Examples of drugs that can be used to control post-operative pain

Diamorphine
Morphine

Pethidine
Omnopon
Fentanyl
Alfentanil
Buprenorphine
Marcain

SMALL VOLUME PORTABLE INFUSION PUMPS

Small volume infusion pumps are particularly versatile because they can be set up on ambulatory as well as bed-ridden patients within both the hospital and the community. They can play an invaluable role in the management of patients with terminal disease.

In all cases these pumps should be used for an indicated clinical problem, for example difficulty in swallowing, gastrointestinal obstruction or intractable pain, unrelieved by oral or intermittent injection therapy.

Inappropriate use of these pumps, when other co-adjuvant therapies or methods of administration are more appropriate, may lead to more difficulty in managing regimes or sites, and less patient compliance when a syringe driver is needed at a later stage.

The Graseby syringe driver

This syringe driver is a battery operated instrument which allows a continuous infusion of drugs in a 10 ml or 20 ml syringe to be administered over a calculated period of time.

Rate of administration
It is important to remember that the volume of solution in the syringe is measured in millilitres, i.e. 'ml'. The rate of delivery from the syringe driver, however, is measured in millimetres, i.e. 'mm'.

Different makes of syringe have different barrel lengths. It is therefore important to check the volume required, i.e. 'ml' against the 'mm' scale on the syringe driver itself prior to the commencement of each new regime (see Fig. 7.1).

Two models of syringe driver in use are the Graseby MS16A and MS26.

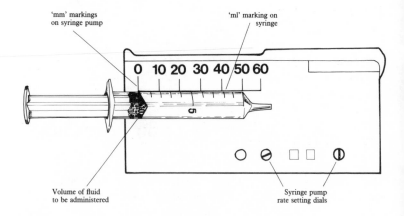

Fig. 7.1 How to measure volume in a syringe (ml) against the length of volume (mm).

The MS16A runs at the rate of mm/h.
The MS26 runs at the rate of mm/24h.

Examples of rate calculation using a 10 ml volume Gillette or Braun Omnifix syringe which measures 50 mm on the syringe driver scale
On first administration of a syringe driver or after having changed the infusion set the line will have to be primed. The volume of fluid that has been used to prime the line should be subtracted from the total volume which is to be used in calculating the rate of administration. This can be done by checking the volume left in the syringe, after priming the line, against the 'mm' scale on the syringe driver. For example, if it takes 2 mm volume to prime a line, the total volume left in a 10 ml syringe will be 50 mm − 2 mm = 48 mm.

MS16A syringe driver
When the line has been newly primed, using the example of 2 mm volume in the dead space, a 24 hour regime is calculated as follows:

$$\frac{\text{Length of volume (mm)}}{\text{Delivery time required (h)}} = \text{rate in mm/h}$$

Therefore: $\dfrac{48 \text{ mm}}{24 \text{ h}} = 2$ mm/h

When only changing the syringe and not priming the line, the total volume in the syringe, i.e. 50 mm, should be adjusted for accurate calculation of the rate to 48 mm or just under 10 ml. It is important to adjust the volume in the syringe up or down as compromise rate settings only allow an approximate duration of infusion, for example, if a full 10 ml syringe (50 mm) was used:

$$\dfrac{50 \text{ mm}}{24 \text{ h}} = 2.133 \text{ mm/h}$$

This has to be rounded down on the rate setting to 2 mm/h.

MS26 syringe driver
When the line has been newly primed, using the example of 2 mm volume in the dead space, a 24 hour regime is calculated as follows:

$$\dfrac{\text{Length of volume (mm)}}{\text{Delivery time required (days)}} = \text{rate in mm/24 h}$$

Therefore: $\dfrac{48 \text{ mm}}{1 \text{ day}} = 48$ mm/24 h

When only changing a syringe and not priming the line the total volume will be 50 mm and no adjustment will be required to the volume:

$$\dfrac{50 \text{ mm}}{1 \text{ day}} = 50 \text{ mm/24 h}$$

In some cases a more dilute solution may be required, for example, using a 20 ml syringe. Exactly the same procedure should be followed as for the 10 ml syringe measuring the syringe volume against the 'mm' scale on the syringe driver prior to the calculation.

Setting up the syringe driver

1. Draw up the required solution in the syringe.
2. Set the calculated rate on the syringe driver.
3. Prime the infusion set with the solution in the syringe.
4. Insert the cannula into the selected site and secure.
5. Insert the battery into the compartment in the syringe driver. The alarm will then sound for a few seconds then fade out. An alkaline battery is preferable, for example a Duracell MN1604. The battery will last for approximately 50 full syringes. The light will stop flashing 24 hours prior to it running out.
6. Fix the syringe onto the syringe driver by:
   (i) Fitting a flange of the syringe into the slot provided on the syringe driver.
   (ii) Secure the syringe firmly with the rubber securing strap.
   (iii) Press the white button on the Actuator Assembly, press this along the lead screw and press it agains the syringe plunger (see Fig. 7.2).

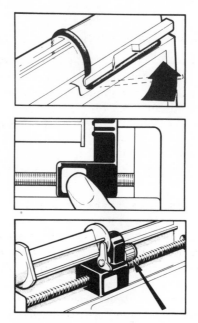

Fig. 7.2 Setting up the syringe driver.

7.   Press the 'start/test' button on the syringe driver. This will run for a few seconds then stop as a check that the motor safety circuits are operating.
8.   Connect the infusion set to the syringe.
9.   Press the 'start/test' button again to operate. The indicator light will flash every second in the MS16A and every 25 seconds in the MS26.
10. Place the syringe driver in the plastic holder and if appropriate place in the shoulder holster to allow free movement of ambulant patients.
11. If appropriate; the 'start/test' button can be pressed on the MS26 model for up to 8.9 seconds at a time to allow a boost of a drug.
12. Should the alarm sound, the following checks should be made:
     empty syringe
     kinked tubing
     blocked needle/tubing
     jammed plunger

The Braun 'Perfusor M' syringe driver

The Braun 'Perfusor M' is a small volume (10 ml) portable infusion pump which has a clockwork mechanism and three pre-set flow rates. The clinical indications for its use and warnings about misuse are the same as for the Graseby syringe driver. Fig. 7.3 illustrates the syringe driver and indicates the use of each component.

Setting up the syringe driver
1.   Draw up the required solution in a 10 ml Braun Omnifix syringe.
2.   Wind the clockwork key clockwise as indicated by the arrow. This will move the metal slot to the right and should be wound until the required distance needed to secure the syringe plunger flange in the metal slot has been reached.
3.   Place the syringe into the syringe driver as illustrated in Fig. 7.3.
4.   Select the flow rate by turning the arrow towards the appropriate number of hours the regime is to run over, i.e. 6, 12, or 24 hours.

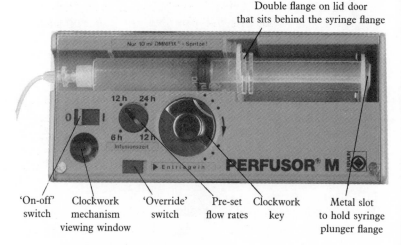

Double flange on lid door
that sits behind the syringe flange

'On-off'   Clockwork   'Override'   Pre-set   Clockwork   Metal slot
switch   mechanism   switch   flow rates   key   to hold syringe
    viewing window   plunger flange

Fig. 7.3   Example of a perfusor pump, 10 ml. Courtesy of B. Braun
Medical Limited.

5.   Switch the 'on–off' switch from 0 to 1. This will activate the
    clockwork mechanism, which can be seen just below the
    switch.
6.   If a bolus is required the 'Entriegein' or 'override' switch
    should be held to the right and the clockwork key turned
    anticlockwise until the required amount has been infused.
7.   Close the lid door, ensuring that the double flange on the lid is
    sitting behind the syringe flange to secure it well in place.

Information and advice should be sought on other small volume
infusion pumps as appropriate so that their suitability can be
assessed for individual requirements.

LARGE VOLUME CONTINUOUS INFUSION PUMPS

In some clinical situations, analgesics and local anaesthetic agents
need to be administered in volumes larger than can practically be
administered via a 10–20 ml small volume infusion pump. For
example:

1. Opiates such as pethidine may require a continuous intravenous infusion to provide effective pain relief in situations such as post-operative pain or sickle cell crisis.
2. Local anaesthetic agents such as Marcain may require a continuous epidural infusion of a given volume and concentration to provide effective pain relief in situations such as post-operative pain, end stage vascular disease including pre- and post-amputation, selected cancer pain syndromes such as some neurogenic pain syndromes and pathological fractures that cannot be surgically corrected. In some cases where the pain is due to a unilateral problem, a more specific plexus infusion of local anaesthetic may be appropriate. For example, a unilateral fractured neck of femur may be treated with a lumbar plexus infusion.
3. The combination of an opiate and a local anaesthetic agent may be useful via the epidural route in situations such as end stage vascular disease, and selected cancer pain syndromes.

There are a great many 30–60 ml infusion pumps available at the present time which run on a ml per hour setting. Advice and information should therefore be sought on variations such as mains and/or battery supply, different sizes, and the facility to check, for example, how many ml have been given and are remaining. Assessment can then be made of the appropriate infusion pump for individual requirements within different clinical situations.

PATIENT CONTROLLED ANALGESIC PUMPS

The facility to allow the patient to be in control of their own pain relief within pre-set safe limits is the aim of a patient controlled analgesic (PCA) pump.

PCA pumps are currently used in clinical situations such as the management of post-operative pain and sickle cell crisis. Their use, however, has the potential to widen as more becomes known about the benefits of using such a system. Each PCA pump has a slightly different combination of options that it can provide. Examples of these options include:

Security coding to enter the system.
Key to lock the pump.
Reservoir or syringe to store the fluid.
Purpose-made priming line.
Automatic line priming.
mg(s)/ml(s) setting.
ml(s)/hour(s) setting.
mg(s)/hour(s) setting.
Basal rate setting.
PCA parameters, including lock-out time between doses.
History feedback, either in-built in the system or a separate printer.

Fig. 7.4 illustrates a PCA pump that requires attachment to a drip pole, and Fig. 7.5 illustrates an ambulatory PCA pump. Advice and information should be sought on the appropriate pump for individual requirements.

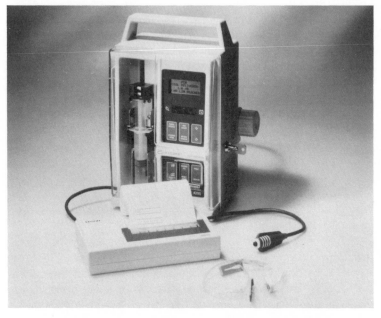

Fig. 7.4 Example of a patient controlled analgesic pump (large, 30 ml). Courtesy of Abbott Laboratories Limited.

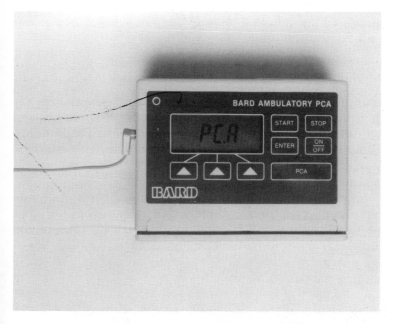

Fig. 7.5 Example of an ambulatory patient controlled analgesic pump. Courtesy of Bard Limited.

BIBLIOGRAPHY

Abbott Laboratories Ltd, Information Booklet.
Bard Ltd, Information Booklet.
B. Braun Medical Ltd, Information Booklet.
Graseby Medical Information Booklet and Chart.
Regnard, C.F.B. and Davies, A. (1986) *A Guide to Symptom Relief in Advanced Cancer.* Haigh and Hochland University Booksellers, Manchester.
Regnard, C.F.B., Pashley, S. and Westrope, F. (1986) Anti-emetic diamorphine mixture compatibility in infusion pumps. *British Journal of Pharmaceutical Practice*, 218–220.
St Christopher's Hospice, *The Syringe Driver* Information Sheet.

Neural blockade 8

Chapter 4 discussed the importance of accurate assessment in deciding the cause of pain, because different types of pain require different treatments. Neural blockade can be an effective treatment when the cause of pain is found to be due to nerve irritation or invasion because nerves can be blocked by using either local anaesthetics or neurolytic solutions.

Historically, neural blockade has been performed by anaesthetists and from this expertise has grown the concept of the pain relief unit. Although there are common principles of neural blockade, each unit inevitably has different ideas about finer details of technique. These are often influenced by factors such as the individual preference of the consultant and the facilities that are available. For this reason the treatments outlined in this chapter are discussed in fairly general terms. Fig.8.1 illustrates some of the sites at which neural blockade is commonly performed.

EPIDURAL INJECTION

An epidural injection can offer effective pain relief in a variety of situations which include:
1. Back pain or referred nerve root pain due to malignant disease such as spinal secondaries.
2. Back pain or referred nerve root pain due to benign conditions such as osteoarthritis and osteoporosis.
3. Post-operative pain.
4. Labour pain during childbirth.
5. Malignant disease requiring opiate and/or local anaesthetic therapy via the epidural route.
6. End stage vascular disease requiring opiate and/or local anaesthetic therapy via the epidural route.

Three methods of administering epidural drugs and their nursing implications are outlined.

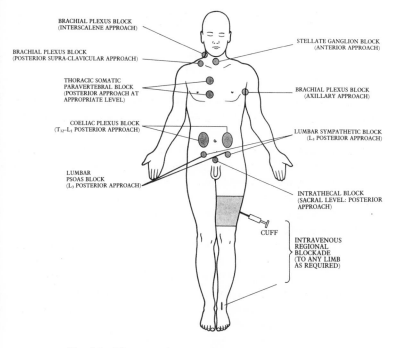

Fig. 8.1 Diagrammatic approaches to common neural blockade.

Single epidural injection

A single epidural injection as near to the level of the pain as possible can be effective in reducing local inflammatory processes. A combination of local anaesthetic and steroid drugs are commonly used. Examples of these drugs are bupivicaine (Marcain) 0.125–0.5% 10 ml and methylprednisolone (Depo-Medrone) 80–120 mg.

For the comfort of the patient intravenous sedation can be administered. This therefore makes the patient more relaxed and facilitates compliance during the procedure. Depending on the clinical situation and facilities available X-ray control may or may not be used.

Nursing responsibilities
- Before the procedure pre-operative preparation and counselling are required.

- During the procedure the nurse will either scrub to assist the doctor or support the patient in the appropriate position which is often with the back flexed and the legs curled up to facilitate introduction of the cannula into the epidural space.
- After the procedure pulse, blood pressure and respiration should be monitored regularly and the doctor informed of any changes such as the blood pressure falling. This is particularly important when local anaesthetic has been injected.

Management of intravenous fluids may be required for some patients.

Bladder function should be monitored and any signs of retention reported.

If local anaesthetic has been used the patient should be reassured that any numbness or weakness is only transient and will wear off gradually.

For the first six hours the nurse should ensure that the patient remains in the appropriate position, which will depend on the level of the epidural. Bed rest should be maintained for 24 hours.

The nurse should reassure the patient as he recovers from the intravenous sedation that may have been given. Reassessment of the pain should be made, including changes in mobility, so that appropriate changes can be made in treatment such as analgesia and physiotherapy.

Temporary epidural catheter

A temporary epidural catheter is inserted to enable bolus administration or continuous infusion of an opiate and/or local anaesthetic.

For more long-term use such as in palliative care situations, the temporary catheter can be tunnelled subcutaneously to the side and sutured. This can reduce the risks of both infection and catheter movement, while avoiding the use of a general anaesthetic for the procedure.

As with a single epidural injection, intravenous sedation can be given for the comfort of the patient and to facilitate the procedure. Intravenous fluids may be required when administering local anaesthetics to maintain the blood pressure.

Nursing responsibilities
Responsibilities before and during the procedure are as for the single injection. After the procedure, observations and monitoring of the patient are as for a single injection. During an acute situation, observations should be carried out every 5 minutes for 15 minutes after each top-up. In between these times while the catheter is in-situ, routine observations should be maintained. Sterile dressings such as op-site should be placed over the site of entry of the catheter into the skin and over the subcutaneous tunnelling site. These dressings should be changed the day after the procedure and then as necessary to keep the sites clean. Any remaining catheter should be taped as required and changed daily to lessen the risk of skin sores. The filter should be changed regularly, or if it becomes blocked.

Any sign of infection around the catheter site itself or surrounding areas should be reported immediately. Doctors have prime responsibility for the administration of epidural drugs although this role falls within the extended role of the nurse. Nurses who can qualify to administer epidural drugs include midwives, nurses specifically trained within pain relief or terminal care units and registered nurses who have undertaken a course recognised by their health authority.

Implanted epidural catheter

A more permanent system which comprises of an indwelling epidural catheter and a subcutaneous reservoir can be surgically implanted. This system can be used for patients who require long-term opiate therapy by the epidural route. Advantages over temporary catheters include reduced risk of infection and movement of the catheter, administration of drugs by a subcutaneous injection into the reservoir, and an increased chance of the patient maintaining a more normal life style within the community.

Nursing responsibilities
- The system is surgically implanted therefore pre-operative preparation and counselling are required.
- After the procedure routine post-operative monitoring and management should be observed.

   Due to the fact the catheter has to be tunnelled and the reservoir implanted subcutaneously small incision sites will have to be dressed and the sutures removed when the sites have healed.

Timing and dosage of drugs will already have been calculated while the temporary catheter was in-situ. However, observations should be made regularly following administration of drugs into the new system until it has been found to be working properly and the patient is in a stable condition.

The aim of the implanted system is to allow the patient an independent life style, so the nurse should educate the patient and his family as appropriate on how to administer a subcutaneous injection and how the system works.

SACRAL INTRATHECAL BLOCK

The sacral intrathecal block can be an effective treatment in the management of distressing problems such as perineal pain due to rectal or pelvic tumour. It is particularly important that the procedure and its risks are discussed with the patient because there is a potential risk of impairing bladder and/or bowel function. This is because the posterior sensory and anterior motor nerves at the sacral level are in very close proximity. The worry of these possible complications is obviously reduced with patients who already have a urinary catheter and/or a colostomy.

To illustrate the benefits that can be gained from the procedure and to gain the confidence of the patient a temporary local anaesthetic block may be advisable in a selected number of patients before considering a more permanent neurolytic block. It should, however, be stressed that each time the procedure is performed with either local anaesthetic or a neurolytic agent the potential risk to bladder and/or bowel function is present. Heavy spinal bupivicaine (Marcain) 0.5% is an example of a local anaesthetic agent, and phenol 7.5% in 50% glycerin is an example of a neurolytic agent. Some patients may choose to continue with more frequently repeated local anaesthetic blocks rather than proceeding with a neurolytic block.

The positioning of the patient both during and for six hours after the procedure is of paramount importance. The patient should be propped back at an angle of 45° to enable the solution to have the maximal effect on the posterior nerve roots. This also helps to reduce the potential risk of impairment of bladder and/or bowel function.

The procedure is usually carried out on the patient's bed and bed rest should be maintained for 24 hours after the procedure.

Intravenous sedation is given to make the procedure more comfortable for the patient and to help the patient remain in the appropriate position after the procedure.

Nursing responsibilities
- Before the procedure routine pre-operative preparation is required.

  The nurse should discuss with and counsel the patient about the procedure, and any questions should be answered as clearly as possible.

  The bed and pillows should be positioned so that the patient does not have to be moved unnecessarily after the procedure.
- During the procedure the nurse should either scrub to assist the doctor or help to support the patient in the appropriate position.
- After the procedure the patient is usually sedated so regular observations of pulse, blood pressure and respiration are required. Bladder and bowel function should be monitored as appropriate.

  During the recovery period the nurse should ensure that the patient remains in the appropriate position and reassures him as he recovers from the intravenous sedation.

  Regular reassessment should be documented of any changes in the pain so that appropriate changes in other treatments, for example gradually reducing analgesic medication if the block is successful, can be made.

COELIAC PLEXUS BLOCK

Neural blockade of the coeliac plexus can be extremely useful in the treatment of symptoms such as pain, nausea and vomiting associated with carcinoma of the upper abdomen, for example primary or metastatic disease of the stomach, liver, pancreas and gall-bladder. The procedure can also be used in the treatment of pain secondary to chronic pancreatitis, but the results are less conclusive in these cases.

The procedure is performed under X-ray control so that the compartment which contains the coeliac plexus at the anterior borders of T_{12}–L_1 can be identified with contrast medium. For diagnostic procedures a local anaesthetic such as bupivicaine (Marcain) 0.5% is injected. For a more permanent block a neurolytic agent such as alcohol 90% is injected. The block can be performed either unilaterally or bilaterally depending on the symptoms to be treated.

Due to the fact that the major sympathetic nerve plexus in the body is being injected intravenous fluids are given during and after the procedure to compensate for any resultant drop in blood pressure. A vasoconstrictor such as ephedrine may also be required. Should the blood pressure drop the head of the bed should never be tipped down as this will allow the alcohol to flow upwards.

Intravenous sedation is given for the comfort of the patient and to facilitate compliance during the procedure. To allow the agent injected to diffuse around the plexus the patient should be as flat as possible for six hours after the procedure. Bed rest should be maintained for 24 hours to allow recovery from the procedure and its resultant effects.

Nursing responsibilities
- Before the procedure pre-operative preparation and counselling are required.
- During the procedure the nurse should either scrub to assist the doctor or help support the patient in the appropriate position, which is usually lying face down on the X-ray table.
- After the procedure the nurse should monitor pulse, blood pressure and respirations quarter hourly for two hours, then gradually reduce if stable.

   Intravenous fluid regimes should be maintained and medication such as ephedrine given as directed.

   The nurse should ensure that the patient remains in the appropriate position and should reassure him as he recovers from the intravenous sedation.

   Regular assessment should be made of any changes in the pain so that appropriate changes in other treatments, such as gradually reducing analgesic and/or anti-emetic medication after a successful block can be made.

LUMBAR SYMPATHETIC BLOCK

Common indications for a lumbar sympathetic block are peripheral vascular disease of the lower limbs, some types of lower abdominal and pelvic pain related to nerve infiltration or irritation and rectal tenesmus associated with pelvic tumour. The procedure is performed under X-ray control so that the compartment which contains the lumbar sympathetic plexus at the anterior borders of L3 can be identified with contrast medium.

For diagnostic procedures a local anaesthetic agent, for example bupivicaine (Marcain) 0.5% is injected. For a more permanent block a neurolytic agent, for example phenol 7.5% in glycerol is injected. The procedure can be performed either unilaterally or bilaterally depending on the symptoms to be treated. Intravenous fluids are not usually given routinely, but as fluid has been injected into the lumbar sympathetic plexus the blood pressure should be monitored in case it should drop. Intravenous sedation is given for the comfort of the patient and to facilitate compliance during the procedure.

To allow the agent injected to settle the patient should lie as flat as possible for six hours after the procedure. Bed rest should be maintained for 24 hours to allow recovery from the procedure and its resultant effects.

Nursing responsibilities
- Before the procedure pre-operative preparation and counselling are required.
- During the procedure the nurse either scrubs to assist the doctor or helps to support the patient in the appropriate position which is usually lying face down on the table.
- After the procedure the nurse should monitor pulse, blood pressure and respirations half hourly for two hours, then gradually reduce if stable. The nurse should ensure that the patient remains in the appropriate position and reassure him as he recovers from the intravenous sedation.

  Regular reassessment should be made of any changes in the pain. When caring for vascular patients the nurse should also assess the warmth and colour of the affected leg and foot. This is to assess the effect of the block on the sympathetic supply to this area.

THORACIC SOMATIC PARAVERTEBRAL BLOCK

Common indications for this procedure are lung or bronchial tumours pressing on the chest wall and thoracic nerves, malignant or benign bone disease causing nerve irritation and invasion and thoracotomy scar pain.

The procedure is performed under X-ray control so that the appropriate level and space can be identified with contrast medium.

For diagnostic procedures a local anaesthetic, for example bupivicaine (Marcain) 0.5% is injected. For a more permanent block a neurolytic agent, for example phenol 7.5% in 50% glycerin is injected. In either case several thoracic segments can be covered by one injection. If repeated top-ups or continuous infusion of local anaesthetic is required a catheter can be inserted. The block can be performed either unilaterally or bilaterally depending on the symptoms to be treated.

Although complications are rare, particularly when performed under X-ray control, it should be noted that due to the proximity of the injection to the lung a pneumothorax is possible. Also intraspinal injection is possible if the injection is too medial. Blood pressure can occasionally fall, particularly if local anaesthetics have been injected.

Intravenous sedation is given for the comfort of the patient and to facilitate compliance during the procedure. The patient should either lie down or sit propped up for six hours after the procedure to allow the agent injected to settle as required. Bed rest should be maintained for at least 12 hours to allow for recovery from the procedure and its resultant effects.

Nursing responsibilities

- Before the procedure pre-operative preparation and counselling are required.
- During the procedure the nurse should either scrub to assist the doctor or help to support the patient in the appropriate position. This is usually face down on the X-ray table.
- After the procedure the nurse should monitor pulse, blood pressure and respiration half hourly for two hours, then gradually reduce if stable.

  The nurse should ensure that the patient remains in the appropriate position and reassures him as he recovers from the intravenous sedation.

Regular reassessment should be made of any changes in the pain so that appropriate changes in other treatments, such as gradually reducing analgesic medication can be made.

LUMBAR PSOAS BLOCK

Symptoms such as a painful hip or knee can be helped by a lumbar psoas block. The procedure can be performed in theatre as a regional block during operation, or can be performed as a therapeutic technique for conditions such as osteoporosis, osteoarthritis, Paget's disease or bone metastases.

X-ray control may be used depending on the clinical situation and facilities available. The procedure is usually performed at the level of L_3 and a local anaesthetic such as bupivicaine (Marcain) 0.5% with or without steroid such as methylprednisolone (Depo-Medrone) 80 mg is injected into the lumbar psoas compartment. If repeated top-ups or continuous infusion of local anaesthetic is required a catheter can be inserted. The block can be performed unilaterally or bilaterally depending on the symptoms to be treated.

As a relatively large amount of local anaesthetic may be injected particular observations of blood pressure should be made in case it should fall. Transient numbness and/or weakness of the lower limb(s) gradually wears off during the initial recovery period if it occurs. The length of relief offered by this procedure is not predictable and appears to be very much an individual response.

Intravenous sedation is given for the comfort of the patient and to facilitate compliance during the procedure. The patient should remain on bed rest for 24 hours after the procedure to allow for recovery from the procedure and any resultant effects.

Nursing responsibilities
- Before the procedure pre-operative preparation and counselling are required.
- During the procedure the nurse may either scrub to assist the doctor or help to support the patient in the appropriate position which will depend on the clinical situation.
- After the procedure the nurse should monitor pulse, blood pressure and respirations half hourly for two hours, then reduce if stable.

The nurse should ensure that the patient remains on bed rest for 24 hours, and reassures him during this period if he is worried by any transient feelings of weakness, and as he recovers from the intravenous sedation.

Gradual mobilisation should be supervised by the nurse and/or physiotherapist.

Regular assessment should be made of any changes in the pain, particularly with reference to improvements and changes associated with mobility.

STELLATE GANGLION BLOCK

Conditions such as post-herpetic neuralgia, acute post-traumatic neuralgia, and tumour causing pain of the head, neck and arm involving distribution from the middle and inferior cervical ganglion can be treated with a stellate ganglion block. This method is not usually successful in the treatment of these problems once they have become chronic syndromes. The procedure is usually performed on an outpatient basis. In some cases, however, the patient may need to be admitted for a course of injections because of the severity of their illness and its debilitating effects, for example an elderly person with acute post-herpetic neuralgia.

Local anaesthetic, for example bupivicaine (Marcain) 0.25–0.5% is injected directly into the stellate ganglion. Neurolytic agents are not generally advised due to the close proximity of vital anatomy. As local anaesthetic only gives temporary relief in some severe cases an indwelling catheter may be considered.

The block is performed on the affected side. Intravenous sedation is not normally given because the procedure itself usually takes under a minute to perform.

The patient should lie as flat as possible with the head back and not talk or swallow during the procedure. Immediately after the procedure the patient should sit up to allow the local anaesthetic to flow downwards, not up to the head.

The patient should be monitored for signs of Horner's syndrome, transient arm weakness, hoarse voice and nasal congestion which would indicate a successful cervical sympathetic ganglion block. No formal observations are usually required after the procedure.

Nursing responsibilities

- The nurse should advise the patient to have someone to take him home or arrange transport if the procedure is to be performed on an outpatient basis.
- The nurse who is going to assist with the procedure should reassure and talk to the patient about the procedure and its possible results as the thought of an injection in the neck can be a frightening idea. This also facilitates patient compliance during the procedure.
- During the procedure the nurse should look after the patient helping to keep the neck and head in the correct position and giving reassurance.
- After the procedure the nurse should sit the patient up immediately and observe for the effects of the block. The nurse should ensure the patient rests quietly until he feels well enough to go home if the procedure is performed as an outpatient.

Reassessment of the pain and any changes should be recorded to facilitate appropriate changes in treatment such as reducing the number of injections or changing the analgesic doses.

BRACHIAL PLEXUS BLOCK

Pain in an arm due to conditions such as disease infiltration of the brachial plexus, for example due to secondary carcinoma or injury of the brachial plexus may be treated with a brachial plexus block.

The procedure is usually performed on an outpatient basis. In some cases, however, the patient may need to be admitted if the patient is felt to be too ill to undergo outpatient treatment, or more intensive monitoring and reassessment of the pain is required.

The brachial plexus can be approached by either the axillary, interscalene or supra-clavicular routes, whichever is the most accessible. Most commonly local anaesthetic, for example bupivicaine (Marcain) 0.5% is used because this only affects the sensory nerves and at most only transient motor weakness is likely. Neurolytic agents such as phenol can be injected for longer term effects, but these also affect motor function leaving the patient with a useless arm. Most patients whilst wanting to get rid of the pain do not like the feeling of a useless arm. An injection of 0.75% bupivicaine (Marcain) can be performed to allow the patient to assess and decide for themselves the advantages and disadvantages of loss of motor function for a short period of time. In some cases an indwelling catheter may be considered.

The patient should sit or lie in a position which is most comfortable for them and also allows greatest accessibility to the approach for the doctor. No formal observations are usually required after the procedure. Due to the proximity of the injection to the lung, pneumothorax can be a complication.

Nursing responsibilities
- The nurse should advise the patient to have someone to take him home after the procedure or arrange transport if outpatient treatment is being given.
- Before the treatment the nurse should reassure the patient and decide with the patient the most appropriate position for the procedure to be performed.
- During the procedure the nurse should position and hold the arm/head of the patient in the required position.
- After the procedure the nurse should ensure that the patient rests quietly until he is ready to go home if it is performed on an outpatient basis. A sling may be required for any transient weakness of the affected arm.

  Regular reassessment of the pain and any other related factors such as changes of mobility of the arm should be noted so that future treatment can be planned.

SPECIFIC JOINT AND TRIGGER AREA BLOCKS

Injections can be performed for localised painful joints such as a facet, shoulder, elbow or knee joint. The same procedure can also be useful for localised painful trigger areas such as post-operative or post-traumatic neuroma formations.

A mixture of local anaesthetic, for example, bupivicaine (Marcain) 0.5%, with or without steriod, for example methylprednisolone

(Depo-Medrone) 40–80 mg is commonly injected to numb the area and reduce any localised inflammation.

Should longer-term therapy be required then cryotherapy, that is freezing of a particular area or nerve, may be useful. The majority of these procedures can be performed on an outpatient basis. Some procedures such as cryotherapy of thoracotomy areas and facet joints, however, may require day case or over-night admission because of the need for light intravenous sedation. X-ray control is usually only required for procedures such as the facet joint injections. Patients who have had procedures performed in close proximity to the lungs, for example, injection or cryoprobing of a thoractomy scar should have a routine chest X-ray prior to leaving the hospital to check that complications such as pneumothorax have not occurred.

Nursing responsibilities
- If the patient is to be given intravenous sedation the nurse should inform the patient not to have anything to eat or drink prior to the procedure. The nurse should also ensure that the patient has someone to take him home or that transport has been arranged, if intravenous sedation is to be given and/or the area to be treated may affect them driving home or going home unattended. The nurse should explain the procedure to the patient and answer any questions the patient may ask.
- During the procedure the nurse should either assist the doctor or help to support the patient in the correct position.
- After the procedure the nurse should routinely monitor pulse, blood pressure and respirations if intravenous sedation has been given and reassure the patient during recovery
- The nurse should ensure that the patient is able to rest quietly until full recovery has been made from the procedure. The patient should be checked to make sure that he is fit to go home.

    Regular reassessment should be made of the pain and if appropriate any related mobility so that future treatment can be planned, for example further procedures, physiotherapy and changes in medication.

INTRAVENOUS REGIONAL BLOCKADE

Some of the common indications for this procedure are sympathetic dystrophy syndrome, causalgia and Raynaud's syndrome. An intravenous cannula is introduced into the affected limb, which is then isolated using a modified Bier's block technique. Intravenous injections are made in varying combinations and doses depending on each individual patient and the limb to be treated.

Examples of drugs used include:

Guanethidine 5–20 mg   a sympathetic blocker
Ketanserin 5–20 mg   a 5-hydroxytryptamine antagonist
Lignocaine 1%   a local anaesthetic
Normal saline 0.9% – to make up the required volume.

The limb should remain isolated for 10–20 minutes to allow the drug to absorb into the affected area. The cuff pressure should then be reduced to allow the blood flow to return to the exsanguinated limb.

The procedure is usually performed on an outpatient basis. Some patients may need to be admitted for intensive treatment in combination with other disciplines such as physiotherapy. Due to the fact that some of the drugs injected act on the sympathetic system, and other drugs used include local anaesthetics, a possible side effect is a drop in blood pressure.

Explanation to the patient that there will be a transient loss of feeling in the affected limb due to exsanguination and the use of local anaesthetic should be given. The patient should also be told to expect changes in colour of the limb during treatment such as a mottled, colourless, bluey arm during exsanguination and a bright red, pink arm as the blood returns to the limb as the cuff is released. A feeling of discomfort may be experienced by the pressure cuff itself around the limb and the blood flowing back into the limb following release of the cuff.

Nursing responsibilities
- The nurse should ensure the patient has someone to take him home or transport arranged if treatment to the limb is likely to affect mobility or the patient has other problems such as existing illnesses.

    The nurse should explain the procedure and its implications to the patient and answer any questions that may be asked.

- During the procedure the nurse should assist the doctor and stay with the patient to reassure him.
- After the procedure, when indicated, the blood pressure should be checked.

The nurse should ensure that the patient rests quietly until the feeling in the limb has returned and recovery has been made from the procedure.

Regular reassessment should be made of the pain and any relevant changes in mobility of the limb so that future treatment can be planned, for example further procedures, physiotherapy and changes in medication.

BIBLIOGRAPHY

Cousins, M.J. and Bridenbaugh, P.O. (eds) (1988) Neural blockade In: *Clinical Anaesthesia and Management of Pain* (2nd edn). J. B. Lippincott, Philadelphia.

Lipton, S. (1984) (ed) *Persistent Pain. Modern Methods of Treatment*, (2nd edn). W.B. Saunders, Philadelphia.

Lipton, S. (1981) *The Control of Pain* Vol.2. Edward Arnold, London.

Transcutaneous nerve   9
stimulation

HISTORICAL BACKGROUND

The concept of electrical stimulation for pain relief is far from modern. The first recorded use was some 2000 years ago by the Roman physician Scribonius Largus. He applied electric eels to haemorrhoids, arthritis, headaches and the feet of gout sufferers.

Although there is some mention of electrotherapy in the middleages, it was not until the early 19th century that the next detailed records appeared. Duchenne de Boulogne developed the earliest known forerunner to the transcutaneous nerve stimulation (TNS) machine in the mid 1830s, using cloth covered electrodes on the skin over the points of entry of the muscular nerves. Faraday developed the electromagnetic generator producing alternating current in 1831. This led to excessive charlatanism and electro-quackery, including claims to cure not only pain, but also such problems as poisoning and sexual impotence!

Researchers and clinicians continued to advance their knowledge of electrical stimulation with the result that by the 20th century, electrical equipment such as the cardiac pacemaker was in clinical use. TNS was introduced into clinical practice following Melzack and Wall's 'gate control theory'.

THE NURSE AND TNS

Nurses within both the hospital and community are in an ideal situation to administer and assess the effects of TNS. They are also in a position to 'tailor-make' the treatment to the patient's needs. TNS can also be coincided very effectively with the work of others trained in its use, for example, physiotherapists. A combined approach to patients in pain can often give the optimum chance of recovery.

The nurse can play an important role in educating the patient in chronic pain how to work the equipment by himself. This in time achieves the goal of a more independent life style which is so important for patients who have suffered from seemingly never-ending and disabling pain.

Nurses should therefore have an overall knowledge in the working of, and clinical indications for TNS, to enable them to practise its application effectively.

HOW DOES TNS WORK?

Gate control theory (see Chapter 3)

This was the original concept underlying the use of TNS in the relief of pain. TNS is thought to play a part in 'closing the gate' by stimulating the large, rapidly conducting fibres within the dorsal horns. This activates inhibition of the small, slowly conducting fibres, and therefore the transmission of pain through the spinal cord.

Stimulation of endogenous opiate release

Another important finding in recent years has been that endogenous opiates, for example encephalins and endorphins, have been found to be present in the mid-brain and laminae I and II of the dorsal horn. Stimulation of these areas has been found to produce analgesic effects.

TNS is thought to stimulate production of these endogenous opiates in laminae I and II of the dorsal horn, therefore inhibiting response of the transmission cells in lamina V to pain signals from an injured area in another part of the body.

THE TNS MACHINE

The TNS machine should be compact so that it can be worn without inhibiting normal everyday activities. However, it should not be so small that the elderly or disabled find it difficult to handle, and particular care should be taken to assess the practical positioning of the controls on different models for each individual patient. The machines are battery-powered, and different models provide the facility to use either one or two pairs of electrodes.

There are three major components of the TNS machine to be considered when discussing how it functions.

Generator

Several combinations of pulses can be produced by a pulse generator. Examples include different widths and frequencies such as continuous high or low frequencies, or intermittent short trains of high frequency pulses delivered at fairly low frequency.

Not all the options, however, are clinically viable when considering their usefulness in the concept of TNS. For example, stimulation at lower frequencies requires higher intensity and can cause painful muscle contraction.

In practice, rectangular pulses (Butikofer and Laurence, 1979) (see Fig.9.1) are simplest to generate, and are satisfactory for delivering a controlled charge to the skin. They also do not show a change in the charge or pulse at different frequencies.

Amplifier

The output is fed into the amplifier where the signal is increased to a level at which sufficient current is delivered to the electrodes.

Impedance of the electrodes, and of the body tissues that separate the electrodes from the peripheral nerve, will determine the amount of current required (for further details see below).

Electrodes

The aim of TNS is to deliver sufficient charge to a pair of electrodes so that the current density produced by the resultant electrical field is able to excite the afferent fibres in an adjacent nerve. This should occur in a controlled manner without damaging the skin.

Impedance of the skin and underlying tissues is very complex and non-homogenous. Differing skin thicknesses and varying frequencies of stimulation can result in significant changes in the impedance (Brennan, 1976). Equally important is the fact that total impedance can change due to changes in the electrodes, e.g. drying electrode gel.

A variety of electrodes are available, for example:

1. The original silicone rubber impregnated with carbon chemicals. These need electrode gel to reduce skin impedance, and also need adhesive tape.
2. Self-adhesive electrodes. These are growing in popularity as prices become more competitive. There are both reusable and disposable types.

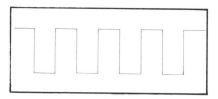

Fig. 9.1 Rectangular pulses.

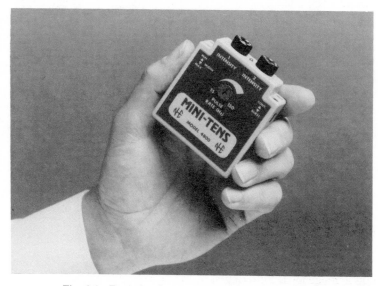

Fig. 9.2 Example of a transcutaneous nerve stimulator. Courtesy of N.H. Eastwood & Son Ltd.

All electrodes, whichever type, should be strong, flexible and inert. They should be at least 4 cm² in size to prevent skin irritation from too high a current density in too small an electrode. Conversely, too large electrodes can deliver insufficient current to stimulate peripheral nerves because of the fall off in current density.

PRACTICAL APPLICATION OF TNS

The typical range of controls are:-

Current 0–50mA (milliampere)
Frequency 0–100 Hz (mean 40–70Hz) (Hertz)
Pulse width 0.1–0.5 ms (millisecond)

Positioning of electrodes

They are usually aligned over the course of a peripheral nerve innervating the painful area. The optimal site is proximal to the pain but TNS can successfully be used distally in some cases, e.g. spinal root pain.

The closer the electrodes are to the nerve, the lower the current needed. This does, however, depend on the thickness of the skin. If stimulation of a large peripheral nerve is not practical, e.g. the sciatic, stimulation of the efferent nerve endings in the immediate vicinity will produce a more localised area of paraesthesia.

Introduction of relief

Unless the patient feels adequate paraesthesia to the site of the pain, it is unlikely that satisfactory pain relief will be achieved. The stimulation should be increased until it is as high as the patient can accept without it being painful or uncomfortable.

The induction time for TNS to produce analgesia ranges from immediately to several hours. The average time is recorded as 20 minutes.

Some patients only get relief during stimulation, others have periods of relief following treatment. Differences most probably reflect the nature of their pain, and the degree of peripheral stimulation achieved. For this reason, the length of time TNS is applied should be tailored to each patient's needs. In chronic pain syndromes there is often a cumulative effect, continuous stimulation producing increasing pain relief over a period of time.

CLINICAL INDICATIONS FOR TNS

Essentially TNS can be used to treat any localised pain, somatic or neurogenic in origin, provided paraesthesia can be generated in the area of the pain. There are, however, diverse views about conditions which can be treated effectively by TNS. A summary is outlined below of some of the more commonly recognised clinical indications (Woolpe, 1984).

Acute pain

Traumatic pain
1. Sports injuries, e.g. torn ligaments, pulled muscles, back strain, etc.
2. Major trauma, e.g. multiple injuries. TNS applied to specific problems, e.g. fractured ribs, in conjunction with lower doses of systemic analgesia, can add to the effectiveness of relief with a lowered incidence of side effects, e.g. respiratory depression.

Post-operative pain
Sterilised electrodes placed adjacent to the incision have been used since the mid 1970s. Since then there have been found to be various levels of effectiveness for abdominal, thoracic, orthopaedic and gynaecological surgery. The advantage, in theory, is that it provides continuous pain relief and reduces the need for narcotics and their side effects.

Labour pain
The treatment should be commenced in the first stage of labour. Two pairs of electrodes are used:

1. One pair at the level of T_{10}–L_1 dermatomes for first stage labour pain.
2. One pair at the level of S_2–S_4 dermatomes for second stage labour pain.

Chronic pain

Pain with neurogenic origin
Peripheral nerve injury
Causalgia
Post-herpetic neuralgia
Amputation
Phantom limb pain
Nerve compression syndromes
Chronic back pain
Joint pains associated with arthritis

Central pain states, e.g. spinal injury
These can be treated but success can only be expected if sufficient paraesthesia can be felt.

Double-blind randomised trials have shown that TNS can be an effective form of treatment in a small percentage of patients suffering from widespread and poorly localised pains, e.g. visceral and psychogenic pain. A major problem is that efficacy of treatment tends to fall off with time in a percentage of patients with chronic pain. This is probably due to a primary placebo effect which falls off very rapidly, while the therapeutic efficacy of TNS tends to fall off more slowly until a stable 20–30 per cent long-term success rate is seen. There does not, however, appear to be any obvious way of predicting which patients in this group will achieve long-term successful pain relief.

COMPLICATIONS AND CONTRA-INDICATIONS

1. The most common problem is allergic dermatitis due to adhesive tape or electrode gel. This can be remedied more easily now with the wide variety of self-adhesive electrodes available.
2. Care should be taken not to place the electrodes in close proximity to vital body areas, e.g. the carotid artery, as electrical stimulation causes excitation of the area.
3. Patients with pacemakers or other implanted electrical devices

which may be affected by the field generated by the stimulator should not use TNS.

4. Patients who cannot understand the controls or implications, e.g. the mentally handicapped, children, or elderly, should not use the machine unless under constant supervision.

    This is because sudden increase in the amplitude control can lead to painful muscle contraction.

REFERENCES

Brennan, K.R. (1976) The characterisation of transcutaneous stimulating electrodes. *IEEE Transactions on Biomedical Engineering*, **23**, 337–340.

Butikofer, R. and Laurence, P.D. (1979) Electrocutaneous nerve stimulation II. Stimulus waveform selection. *IEEE Transactions on Biomedical Engineering*, **26**, 69–74.

Melzack, R. and Wall, P.D. (1989) *The Challenge of Pain*. Penguin, Harmondsworth.

N.H. Eastwood & Son Ltd information booklet. Each manufacturer of TNS has a guide to the background and use of their machines.

Woolpe, C.J. (1989) Transcutaneous and implanted nerve stimulation. In: *Textbook of Pain* (eds. Wall, P.D. and Melzack R.) (2nd edn) Churchill Livingstone, USA. pp. 684–686.

BIBLIOGRAPHY

Melzack, R. and Wall, P.D. (1982) *The Challenge of Pain*. Penguin, Harmondsworth.

N.H. Eastwood & Son Ltd information booklet.

Each manufacturer of TNS has a guide to the background and use of their machines.

Useful Addresses

Hospice Information Service. St Christopher's Hospice.
A resource and link for members of the public and health care professionals. Telephone and written enquiries welcome. It also publishes a directory of hospice/home care/support teams within the UK and Republic of Ireland.

Halley-Stewart Library. Library and Study Bookshop. Librarian — Barbara Greenall.
St Christopher's Hospice
51/59 Laurie Park Road
London SE26 6DZ
Telephone: 081–778–9252

The Lisa Sainsbury Foundation.
8/10 Crown Hill
Croydon
Surrey CRO 1RY
Telephone: 081–686–8808
For information on books, videos and workshops.

The Intractable Pain Society of Great Britain and Ireland.
c/o The Association of Anaesthetists
9 Bedford Square
London WC1B 3RA
For information on Pain Clinics throughout the UK.

Bath Institute of Medical Engineering.
Wolfson Centre
Royal United Hospital
Bath BA1 3NG
Telephone: 0225 823237
The Department of Health Official Evaluation Centre for infusion equipment in the UK.

Index